How's The Viz?

Volume 1

Godly "Visionals" For Men
- To Lift Your Vision Higher.

Dave MacLean

For all the valiant, courageous, ordinary Jesus - following men who everyday keep pressing on to appropriate all that our Lord has accomplished for us.

Well done.

Soli Deo Gloria

TABLE OF CONTENTS

ACKNOWLEDGEMENTS

There are a select few I want to thank for this extraordinary journey I have been on for the last decade. To my Band of Brothers – Stephen, Ben and Brad – thank you for choosing to stay in the adventure amidst the beauty and the brokenness. To John – thank you for being the catalyst for this epic adventure. To Brian – thank you for working with me to get "How's The Viz?" started over 6 years ago.

To my valiant sons David and Benjamin who help adjust my Viz on a regular basis.

Thank you to my precious wife Anne, whose love and prayer support and empower me far more than I have the capacity to comprehend.

Thank you to all the courageous men who have attended our Band of Brothers Boot Camps & Wholehearted Men's events searching for more of the God-Breathed wholeheartedness that Jesus promised us. It has been a great privilege and pleasure to see you come to life and stand up on your feet together, a vast army.

INTRODUCTION

You may be asking yourself, "What's with the title of this book – what does it mean?" Well, "How's The Viz?" is actually a scuba diving term. It is a question you ask other divers who are coming out of the water into which you are about to dive. It's the short form of "How is the visibility?" The question is simply an enquiry into how far you can see. Visibility underwater can vary drastically based on a number of factors. Sometimes you can see quite a good distance, and other times you may not be able to see much farther than the length of your arm.

Life can be like that sometimes can't it? Some days we are full of faith and hope and we seem to be able to see forever. Sadly though, most days are not like this and we oftentimes feel we really don't know what is going on. What is God up to? We can start to lose our perspective and begin to live a very small story, not seeing the greatness of all that God has called us into.

There is a very real and calculated strategy from the enemy of our souls to keep us living a very small story, intended to keep us from apprehending that for which we have been apprehended by God. Most men, however, do not recognize and understand the strategy of the enemy set against them and, therefore, do not experience the life that God has for them. How's The Viz? is designed to encourage, equip and empower you to overcome the strategy of the enemy set against you and apprehend the heart of your Heavenly Father for you.

This book is a collection of weekly e-visionals I send out to Christian men through my ministry Wholehearted Men. My desire is that these e-visionals will help lift your vision higher, to help you see more clearly the nature of the epic adventure into which Jesus has invited you. We need to get our eyes off of ourselves and our own limitations and see the greatness of God.

In order to truly transform your "viz" I suggest you not only read and prayerfully ponder these visionals, but that you also memorize and mediate on the scriptures included in each one. Scripture is the Truth that we must stand on, the eyes of faith through which we must see and the reality in which we must live in the midst of the issues of everyday life.

My desire is to somehow facilitate the breath of God breathing on the dry bones of men's lives to see them come alive and stand up on their feet, together as a vast army for good. This passion is based on Ezekiel 37 and the story of the valley of dry bones. My prayer is that the Lord will breathe life into you so the eyes of your heart will be opened to see all the hope, riches and power that God has given us as beloved sons of our heavenly Father.

"I pray that the eyes of your heart may be enlightened in order that you may know the hope to which He has called you, the riches of

His glorious inheritance in His holy people, and His incomparably great power for us who believe."
Ephesians 1:18-19

Strength and courage,

Dave

More information on Dave's work can be found at the following websites:

www.Wholeheartedmen.com

www.Wholeheartedleaders.com

HOW'S THE VIZ?

So there I stood in my scuba gear, waist deep in the Pacific waters of the Gulf Islands, waiting with my instructor as he talked with another diver who was just coming out of the water. I didn't hear much of their conversation except for the initial question my instructor had asked:

"How's the viz?"

What the heck did that mean?

I soon learned that in Scuba lingo, "How's the viz?" means: "How is the visibility? How far can you see?" You see, the visibility in water can change quite significantly due to currents, tides, rain, temperature, etc. Before you begin a dive it is helpful to know how far you will be able to see – 2 feet, 50 feet, 100 feet?

I've learned over the years that life is like that. Some days it feels like we can see forever. We see the big picture. We're full of faith and hope. *If only everyday were like that...* Many days, if not most days, we feel like we're stuck in cloudy waters. We can't see very far. We don't know what's up ahead, or all around us. We don't really understand our place in the bigger picture. It can be very disorienting. It can even be terrifying.

However, I believe God wants to open up the eyes of our hearts so that we can see the hope of our calling, the riches of our inheritance and His power that He has for us. Sometimes the waters will be clear, sometimes the waters will be cloudy, but if we're able to see with the eyes of our heart – with eyes of faith – our vision can be clear in the midst of our surroundings regardless of how certain or uncertain they may be.

These "e-visionals" are written to help improve your vision and help you begin to see clearly with the eyes of your heart; to help you see the truth of who God is, who He says you are, and the truth about this life into which we are invited. My prayer is that *"How's The Viz?"* will help open the eyes of your heart so that you can, "… see the hope to which He has called us, the riches of His glorious inheritance in us and His incomparably great power for us who believe…".

Ephesians 1:18, 19

"I pray that the Lord may open the eyes of your heart that you might see the hope to which He has called us, the riches of His glorious inheritance in the saints and His incomparable great power that is at work in us."

20 SECONDS OF COURAGE

"We bought a zoo!"

I recently watched this movie on a flight from Chicago to Seattle. It was great. It's the true story of a man with a teenage son and a young daughter who buys a run down, dilapidated zoo.

He has spent his career as a newspaper writer engaging in unique stories which enable him to pursue his passion for casual adventure. He pops in and out of adventurous and adrenaline filled scenarios to create great stories, then returns to his suburban life of bliss. All of this comes crashing down when his beloved wife, the heart, soul and adhesive of his life, is suddenly gone. He now finds himself unable to deal with the critical adventure of fathering his children – particularly his wounded and angry son - and building a life together. He is wounded, mourning and feeling completely ill-equipped for life. He needs a new beginning. They need a new beginning. They need something to bring them together as a family.

Enter the idea of moving and buying a new house. Simple. However, one thing leads to another and instead of buying a new house in a new neighbourhood he buys a home on an 18 acre property outside of town and...a zoo. The adventure begins: leading a staff, caring for animals, healing his heart, reaching out to his son to restore their relationship and heal his son's heart, helping his young daughter get her happiness back, and pouring lots of

3

money, hard work and emotional energy into saving a dilapidated zoo in need of recertification in order to welcome paying customers once again.

This new life demands courage on all fronts, every day. He says something in the movie that was very powerful and caught my attention: when facing particularly intimidating and fear-filled situations, "...all you need is 20 seconds of insane courage...20 seconds of embarrassing bravery...that's all you need...and something great will come of it."

In other words, when confronted with situations that cause us to be afraid, we don't need to be fearless and completely brave - we simply need to choose courage for 20 seconds. 20 seconds will be enough to get you into something that you probably can't get out of and now have to see it through.

Courage is not a gift. It's not an ability. It's not a skill. Courage is a choice. It is an act of your will. Fear always precedes courage; therefore, fear is a prerequisite for being courageous. If you are not afraid, you don't need courage. And, if you are not afraid, then you are probably not in an adventure that demands more of you than you realize you have - one in which God can make up the difference. If you are afraid and intimidated then you are perfectly positioned to live courageously, you simply need to choose 20 seconds of courage and move forward.

Jump in. Let go. Open up. Reach out. Hold on. Don't stop. Speak up. Stand up. Get up. Whatever you are facing, choose 20 seconds of courage and go for it. 20 seconds of courage will engage you and get you in the game; Jesus can then see you through if you keep going and receive His grace to do what needs to be done.

Following Jesus into this epic adventure called life in the Kingdom of God demands courage. In fact, cowardice prevents us from walking with Him into that which He is calling us. Cowardice is simply giving into fear and not moving forward. We must take courage in order to live the life for which Jesus has created, crafted and called us.

Good news though: you can be courageous. You can take courage. Anyone can be courageous for 20 seconds – that's all it takes to get you in the game. Start encouraging yourself to choose 20 seconds of courage when you feel afraid or intimidated and I believe you will find yourself living more of the adventure that you thirst for. And, you will become bolder and more courageous than you thought possible.

Go for it – 20 seconds of courage. You can do that. And, great things will come of it.

I Corinthians 16:13
"Be on your guard; stand firm in the faith; be courageous; be strong."

Acts 27:25

"So keep up your courage, men, for I have faith in God that it will happen just as He told me."

Matthew 14:27

"But Jesus immediately said to them: "Take courage! It is I. Don't be afraid.""

Joshua 1:9

"Have I not commanded you? Be strong and courageous. Do not be afraid; do not be discouraged, for the LORD your God will be with you wherever you go."

A BAD IMITATION

I saw Elvis. Yup, clear as day.

I was walking through a hotel in Las Vegas when suddenly a wall began to roll up to reveal Elvis in all his glory. There he was on stage swaggering about, crooning away and throwing sweat soaked scarves into the audience. Women were charging the stage to grab hold of this unique piece of Elvis memorabilia. The men, who had been presumably dragged to the show by their significant female others, were enjoying the sight of Elvis' flamboyant Vegas show girl back-up singers. The roll up wall was a unique promotional tactic to give passers by a glimpse into the tail end of the show to entice us to purchase tickets to see Vegas' number one Elvis impersonator.

I must say, I stood there with a colleague and watched the entire conclusion of the show. I was curious, captivated, stupefied and speechless. What a spectacle. The band pounded out the final two songs with show stopping power. The entire extravaganza was building up to this final climax in an attempt to work the audience up into an Elvis fueled frenzy of crazy, over-the-top showmanship.

"Thank you. Thank you very much."

The crowd went crazy with applause. This guy must have put on quite the show – people seemed to love it. If nothing else he sure worked up a sweat.

One of the final songs he sang was "Caught in a Trap". I thought to myself, "You can say that again." This guy has spent his entire life pretending to be someone else. Hey, Elvis was quite extraordinary I have no qualms about that. However, is Elvis worth impersonating with your entire life? This guy is billed officially as an Elvis impersonator. That's all he does. He does a good imitation, but of the wrong person.

I think we all imitate others to a certain degree. There are many people in our lives – past and present – whom we admire and we want to be like. Who do you want to be like? Do you want to be like the guy with all the money, the high paying important job, the fancy car, the big house, the exotic travel and the trophy wife? Do you admire the things of this world and those who seem to have achieved success in worldly terms? Or, do you want to be like the man who walks closely with Jesus and gives himself wholeheartedly to God's kingdom in him and through him. Do you want to imitate God and godliness in other men?

Paul exhorts us to be imitators of God. He even encourages the Corinthians to be imitators of him. We all learn from other people. Other people can be good examples for us. We can have mentors in our lives who serve as good examples - we want to be like them. We want to have similar character qualities as the people we admire. In a sense, we are imitating them. I know there are men in my life who I greatly admire - men who I want to be like. Men who I want to imitate. I don't want to be them. I simply want to have similar character qualities.

Let's not be imitators of the world and follow the pattern of this world. Let's be imitators of good, imitators of God.

III John 11

"Dear friend, do not imitate what is evil but what is good. Anyone who does what is good is from God. Anyone who does what is evil has not seen God."

A BUCKET LIST

Do you have a bucket list?

A bucket list is a list of all those things you want to do or experience before you die – before you "kick the bucket". My son asked me the other day what was on my bucket list. I thought, "Gee, I don't really have a formal list of anything – hmmmm."

So, I asked him what is on his bucket list:

- Go skydiving
- Run with the bulls in Spain
- Go "Noodling"
- Fly in a fighter jet
- Learn to speak Spanish fluently
- Cage diving with great white sharks
- Climb a mountain over 20,000 ft.
- Wear a suit of armour
- Etc., etc., etc.

Wow, this was quite the list. I put it down to youthful enthusiasm and was encouraged that he has lots of hopes and dreams – even over and above his bucket list. I began to consider my lack of hopes and dreams: my bucket list. Hey, I have had a pretty cool life so far, filled with many fabulous experiences. Can I really expect the latter years of my life to be filled with as much or more than the earlier years of my life?

A little phrase I heard years ago kept running through my mind. "If I don't believe my best years are yet to come, then my heart has already been taken out."

Am I already resigning myself to a latter life of mediocrity? Has my heart been taken out?

I asked Anne if she has a bucket list. Yes, she has a list of things she would still like to experience before she dies:

- Visit Auschwitz
- Learn to speak Spanish fluently
- Sing Handel's Messiah in a choir
- Visit Spain
- Be in Ottawa on Canada Day
- Etc., etc., etc.

Wow, again I found myself wondering if I was choosing not to live in desire and not to step out into the greatness and grandness of God. C.S. Lewis once said that the problem was not that we desire too much, but that we desire too little. I do not want to desire too little, and as Thoreau said, "...to reach the end of my days and discover that I had not really lived."

We serve a great and good God. He has wonderful plans and purposes for our lives and He also puts desires in our hearts - desires that are part of His glory in us and through us. Now, the world, the enemy and our flesh can also put desires in our hearts, so we need to prayerfully consider our desires and offer them to God with an open hand as an act of worship. "Lord, I would love to be able to... (do this or that) and I offer it to you. Help me to partner with You to experience all that is in Your heart for me and through me."

So, I am starting to assemble a bucket list of sorts – if for no other reason than to stay in desire:

- See an angel and know it
- Facilitate the breath of God breathing on the dry bones of men's lives
- Have a vision of Jesus
- Fly in a fighter jet
- Write at least 2 books
- Speak to young people at Bible and ministry schools around the world
- Have a yacht moored in Vancouver to cruise the coastal waters of BC
- To bring the message of the Father heart of God to the fatherless around the world
- To see my sons married and my grandchildren born
- Go on an African safari
- Etc., etc., etc.

There is far more in God's heart for us than we realize. May we all walk closely with Him in what is in His heart and the desires He puts in our hearts. Don't resign yourself to less than all that is in His heart for you.

Do not desire too little. Dare to put together a bucket list and offer it to Him.

Psalm 37:4

"Delight yourself in the Lord and He will give you the desires of your heart."

I Corinthians 2:9

"...'No eye has seen, no ear has heard, no mind has conceived what God has prepared for those who love Him.'"

A CHANGE OF FAITH

What?

What do you mean I didn't get the job?

It was mine – they all wanted me to be there. It was perfectly suited to me.

How could God do this?

That simple announcement began a change of faith in me. You see, I began to realize that my faith was in "what God would do", not in "who God is".

Let me explain...

I had graduated from UBC, got married, went to Bible School, moved to Winnipeg to be with my brother and the church in Winnipeg, and was working in business as an Account Executive. However, I had always believed that the Lord wanted me to teach, so I resigned from my position and went back to university to get my teaching degree. For my final practicum I was teaching Phys. Ed., Business and History at a high school. I had already volunteered at this school for 3 years coaching the football team, so the kids, and the Athletic Director, knew me.

For my business course I brought in a former client – the founder of Dickie Dee Ice Cream – who put on a seminar on Entrepreneurship, and gave away free ice cream. And, the history teacher who I was working with was retiring that year. All three of the teachers I was working with went to the administration and asked for me to be hired. "Don't lose this kid." "Whatever you have to do, do it and hire him." The history teacher even told the admin to hire me to replace him. So, I thought I was a shoe in for a job at this school.

But God had other plans.

I ended up substitute teaching for 6 months before I got a term contract. My heart still jumps when I hear a certain kind of phone ring. However, this was all part of an elaborate divine plan to shift my faith to more solid ground. I think we all know that God doesn't always do what we think He should. That's why our faith needs to be in "who He is" not what we think He will do. We must know that no matter what the circumstances may be, He remains the same. He is gracious, compassionate, slow to anger, love, truth, life, eternal, immortal, invisible, infinite, merciful, generous, spirit, omniscient, omnipotent, omnipresent and immutable. We can always trust in His great goodness and His good greatness, even though what we see doesn't make sense. One day it will.

Make sure your faith is built on the rock of who Jesus is. Who He is doesn't change.

Hebrews 13:8
"Jesus Christ is the same yesterday and today and forever."

A FAITHFUL TOOL

Do you have a favourite tool?

I think every man probably has a favourite tool: a chainsaw, a weed-eater, a lawnmower, a crescent wrench, vice grips, etc. – that special tool you simply enjoy using. You just feel good when you are done the job, because the tool does such a good job. You know that great feeling of satisfaction you get when you have done a good job well, and your trusty tool helped you get it done with no issues.

I have a tool like that – my blower. I have a Husqvarna 2-stroke, back pack, high capacity blower that I just love using. I put on my ear gear, lock the throttle on full and start blowing. I use it to clean the patio, the deck, the drive way, the pool area; I even use it to "rake" leaves in the fall.

I recently pulled it out for the first time this spring after winter. You never know how well a gas powered tool is going to fire up after winter, so I wasn't sure if I was going to have to do a little work on it to get it going. Each of my gas-powered tools has a different sequence I go through to get it started. With the blower it's: make sure the on/off switch is on, lock the throttle on slightly, flick the choke on, pump the carburetor pump until full, pull the pull cord to crank it over, when it fires I flick off the choke and pull it again. It starts with two pulls every time.

Sure enough, my old faithful tool started up after two pulls. I love this tool! In fact, I even said, "I love you" to my blower. I know, I know, "...though shalt not make any idols..." (Thank you, Jesus, for my blower). I started thinking about my blower and how it is such a faithful tool that I can always count on to get the job done. Sure, I do some maintenance from time to time, but it is just so reliable and faithful.

In light of this I began to ask questions of myself, "Lord, am I a faithful and reliable tool in Your hand, like my blower is in mine?" "Can You depend on me to get the job done like I can depend on my blower?" "Do I partner with You in the work you have for me to do with the same degree of effectiveness as my blower?" "Can others depend on me to work with them the way that I can depend on my blower?"

I really don't think I am as faithful as my blower. I certainly don't start up as effortlessly when the Lord asks me to do things. I whine a little. I complain a little. I come up with reasons why it's not a great idea. I'm kind of tired and need a rest. I want to sit on the shelf a little longer. It's hard work to do the Lord's work and it's not often comfortable and convenient...

However, I want to be a faithful tool in the Lord's hand. I want to be the kind of man that He can depend on to do the work that He wants done, when He wants it done.

Do you want to be that kind of man?

He has invited you and me to partner with Him in the exciting work of the Kingdom. Each of us brings a different skill set and gifting to His work. He needs all of us to do the work that He has invited us to do with Him. It's been said that "Without God we cannot, and without us God will not." He has invited and called you to partner with Him in the work of the Kingdom as a special tool in His hand to do a unique job He has created for you – for the benefit of others.

Offer yourself. Serve others. Partner with Jesus in His work in you and through you. Think of your favourite tool and be like it.

Be a faithful tool in the Lord's hand.

Ephesians 2:10
"For we are God's workmanship, created in Christ Jesus to do good works, which God prepared in advance for us to do."

I Peter 4:10
"Each one should use whatever gift he has received to serve others, faithfully administering God's grace in its various forms."

I Corinthians 15:58
"Therefore, my dear brothers stand firm. Let nothing move you. Always give yourself fully to the work of the Lord, because you know that your labour in the Lord is not in vain."

A GOOD IMITATION

Rolex, Breitling, TAG, Cartier, Movado – high end watch brands. Some guys are really into watches. Some guys wear their watch as a status symbol to make themselves feel important or significant. Some guys don't think twice about their watch – it's simply worn for utilitarian purposes.

I read an article in an inflight magazine about watches. It stated that an entry level watch should cost $100 - $1,000. A mid-range watch should cost $1,000 - $10,000. And, a high end watch should cost more than $10,000. I was dumbfounded. My scale would be something like this: Entry level - $1-$50. Mid-range - $50-$200. High end - $200-$500. You've got to be kidding me range - $500+.

Now I must confess that my family heritage is Scottish, so that tends to skew my willingness to spend money. I still have my good old Timex Ironman that I bought years ago for $36. Not too fashionable, but it works great.

However, recently I started to notice some pretty cool looking watches and thought that I wouldn't mind owning a decent watch for a more classy business look. So, it was with a certain degree of excitement that I found myself at a watch vendor on the streets of Bangkok.

Bangkok is fairly well known as a hot spot to purchase knock offs – imitations, replicas - of all sorts. We were in Bangkok at the tail end of a mission trip to Cambodia. I began the dance with the vendor…

We started looking at all the watches she had displayed on her table. I looked at TAGs and Rolexes, but the one that caught my eye was the Breitling. Now this is a cool looking watch. Classy, classic, sophisticated, yet sporty and adventurous. Wow, this watch was just like me. Yes, this was the look.

She asked me what quality I wanted. You see, there are poor quality imitations and there are high quality imitations. I wanted the best quality. So, she began to dig out a wide variety of high quality Breitling imitations. I ultimately chose the Breitling Navitimer – first introduced in 1952.

Here is how the Navitimer is described on the Breitling website: "In over 50 years of existence the Navitimer has achieved cult object status, thereby joining the select circle of modern, ultra functional and timeless objects that have made their mark on the 20th century." Wow, and I got all the panache of a $5,000 watch for $70 - after significant negotiations.

This interaction started me thinking. I remembered that Paul exhorted us to be imitators of God. I don't think he was encouraging us to be cheap imitations; posers, simply pretending to be godly. No, he was encouraging us to be high quality replicas of God. We cannot become God, but through the powerful regenerating work of the Holy Spirit we can become more and more godly. We can choose to imitate God – to set Him as our example – to strive to become more like Jesus. Or, we can choose to imitate something or someone else. Do you want to be like Jesus, or have you wanted to be like someone else?

Who are you imitating? Let's be true imitators of God – high end replicas transformed by the power of the Holy Spirit.

Ephesians 5:1

"Be imitators of God, therefore, as dearly loved children and live a life of love, just as Christ loved us and gave Himself up for us as a fragrant offering and sacrifice to God."

A GOOD JOB

"Work hard until the job is done."

This is our family definition of what doing "a good job" is. Of course, quality standards are inferred – if you have not met the quality standards that were set for the job, then you are not done.

We believe that a good work ethic is a critical character quality we need to build into our sons. They must know how to work hard and not expect any free rides. I am not talking about a "works" mentality without any understanding of grace. I am simply talking about young men who know how to work hard and get the job done – no whining, no self-pity, no "this is too hard' attitude – hunker down and work hard until the job is done.

Well, this summer that character quality was put to the test in a big way with David and Benjamin, and their buddy Alex from Winnipeg, when they all worked in a cherry processing plant. They started working mid-July and finished up at the end of August. You have about 6 weeks to harvest and ship all the fruit. These cherries are shipped from the plant all over the world – China, Japan, Thailand, France, etc.

You can't dilly dally during harvest – you have to get the job done in a certain amount of time. So, the guys would leave the house at 7 AM, drive 45 minutes to the plant, work like men all day and return home around midnight or later. They would then make lunches for the next day, go to bed and do it all again – 7 days a week. They would work 14 hours a day for days on end. And, they worked in the cooler at the plant so every day, when it was over 30 degrees Celsius outside, they would dress for work in long johns, winter jackets, toques and gloves.

Over the course of a little over 40 days they worked close to 500 hours. They were pushed to their limits and beyond. They had to dig deep for all the strength, energy, motivation, and perseverance they could muster to do a good job. They had to lean on each other to keep going. Over 25 guys started out the season in the cooler and by the end there were only 5 of the original guys left. The others had been fired or quit because it was too hard.

I was so impressed with their work ethic – I don't think I could have done that when I was their age. Wow, I am so proud of them.

We sat down late on Alex's last night before he went back to Winnipeg, talking about the summer and some lessons learned. Recognizing that they had more strength than they thought, more ability to press on and press through – to persevere – than they thought, were big lessons. But Alex shared another profound lesson he learned:

He learned that he could choose his attitude in the midst of hardship. The emotional path of least resistance is to shut down and simply "endure" the process. He said that he learned he could choose a different attitude if he chose to care and invest his heart into his work, his co-workers, his worship through work. He didn't have to just endure things – He could find God's heart in the midst of difficult circumstances and enjoy the journey.

One of the things that made this possible for Alex was the community and camaraderie he shared with David and Benjamin, but also the love, support and encouragement he got from his dad via phone calls and texts in the midst of a particularly difficult time. He learned to rise above his hardship by choosing not to simply endure, but find God in the journey.

Wow, these young men grew up in new ways this summer and worked like men. They also chose to live like men in the midst of the hardship, tapping into a strength and encouragement the Lord had for them.

Now that's a good job.

Proverbs 6:10, 11
"A little sleep, a little slumber. A little folding of the hands to rest – and poverty will come on you like a bandit and scarcity like an armed man."

Proverbs 10:5
"He who gathers crops in summer is a wise son, but he who sleeps during harvest is a disgraceful son."

Isaiah 40:29-31

"He gives strength to the weary and increases the power of the weak. Even youths grow tired and weary, and young men stumble and fall, but those who hope in the Lord will renew their strength, they will soar on wings like eagles, they will run and not grow weary, they will walk and not be faint."

A GOOD TRADE

Do you want what's in the Box, or what's behind the Curtain? Which one will you choose?

Monty Hall would wait patiently – sometimes baiting the contestants – as they hummed and hawed and listened to the shouts of the audience to try and decide what to do. Door #1, Door #2, or Door #3? Will you trade what you have already won for what's behind the door?

Or, there would be a tray carried into the audience and displayed by the lovely Carol Merrill. Will you trade the $100 Monty just gave you for what's under the box on the tray with Carol? The whole trade up scenario may very well have started with Monty walking up to a contestant and offering her $100 for a tube of lipstick in her purse.

Contestants would come to the studio dressed up in crazy costumes in an attempt to capture Monty's attention to encourage him to deal with them. The whole concept to the show was based on the opportunity to trade what you already have for something that could be far more valuable, or it could turn out to be a "Zonk" – something worthless. The studio audience members were all potential contestants who vied for the opportunity to trade for some fabulous prizes and perhaps compete for the "Big Deal of the Day" – trips, cars, jewelry, furniture, electronics, etc.

Yes, Let's Make a Deal was very popular. In fact, it was the most popular game show on TV from 1963 – 1977. I think the show spoke to a deep desire in the human heart to trade something of little value for something of far greater value. To be offered something of worth in exchange for something seemingly worthless. The only hitch on the show was that you didn't know what you were trading for – would it be more or less valuable?

This is a little like what God offers us. Don't get me wrong, God isn't a divine Monty Hall; He doesn't want to make a deal with us and perhaps trick us. No, He simply offers a trade – our trash for His treasure.

What? You can't be serious. My trash for His treasure? Yes, it's true. God offers us treasure in exchange for our trash. Beauty for ashes. Joy for mourning. Praise for heaviness. Healing for wounding. Freedom for imprisonment. Life for death. This is good news – that's why it's called "The Gospel".

Jesus is offering you a trade. Trade the trash of your heart: hopelessness, wounding, defeat, depression, rage, oppression, heaviness, sadness, bitterness, resentment, etc., for the life that He has for you. This is why He came. He offers His abundant life for your empty life. Give Him your life and ask Him to give you His life.

Don't hold onto your trash – give it to Jesus. It's a good trade.

Isaiah 61:1-5

"The Spirit of God, the Master, is on me because God anointed me. He sent me to preach good news to the poor, heal the broken hearted, announce freedom to all captives, pardon all prisoners. God sent me to announce the year of his grace – a celebration of God's destruction of our enemies – and to comfort all who mourn in Zion, give them bouquets of roses instead of ashes, messages of joy instead of news of doom, a praising heart instead of a languid spirit." (The Message)

A LIFE OF REPENTANCE

I had the pleasure and privilege of golfing Pebble Beach a while ago - one of the greatest golf courses in the world. Spectacular scenery, challenging holes: an incredible experience. And, you know what? I shot par. Yup, I shot par at Pebble Beach. Pretty amazing, eh?

Now, before you go thinking that I am an amazing golfer I need to tell you more of the story. I didn't play Pebble Beach at Pebble Beach. I played Pebble Beach at a hotel in Seattle - on their golf simulator. I chose to play Pebble Beach out of more than 50 golf courses from around the world. If you haven't tried out one of these simulators, they are quite extraordinary. You hit off of artificial grass towards a huge video screen that projects computer graphics of the course accurately simulated through the use of GPS. The computer is able to calculate the distance and direction of your shot as you watch the trajectory of your ball on the screen. Your ball lands, you check the hole coordinates on the screen, pick a club and hit again. I found putting the real tricky part, but you know what they say, "Drive for show, putt for dough."

There was one other part of the computer simulation that was particularly helpful for me to shoot par. It's called the Mulligan button. After every shot I had the choice of keeping my shot, or pressing the Mulligan button on the computer screen and shooting another shot. I could choose to not have that stroke counted against me in my game.

I loved that button. I must have pressed that button over 100 times. I would hit a shot that I wasn't pleased with, press Mulligan, adjust my grip, my stance, my angle, and then hit again. I did this over and over again until my shots started to get truer and farther and I needed the Mulligan button less.

As I was doing this I began to think that this is like repentance. In life I do something that isn't good – my shot goes astray. So, I ask the Lord to forgive me and to help me to change – to hit truer next time. Then I take some sort of action to ensure that next time I "hit that shot" I get a better outcome. You see, we are called to a life of repentance. Repentance is a daily choice – a daily gift from the Lord to start again. It's an ongoing gift of mercy and grace from the Lord to lay aside the sin that besets us and keep moving forward in the game of life.

Choose to live a life of continual repentance – an ongoing attitude to lay aside the sin that trips us up and press on toward God's heart for us.

Hebrews 12:1

"Therefore, since we are surrounded by such a great cloud of witnesses, let us throw off everything that hinders and the sin that so easily entangles, and let us run with perseverance the race marked out for us."

A SONG IN THE NIGHT

…387, 388, 389, 390, 391…

I had resorted to this – I was counting my steps. Yup, here I was in some of the most glorious Canadian backcountry that Jesus spoke into existence, lost in the midst of my discomfort and counting my steps to just get through.

My son Benjamin and I were on a backcountry hike with a small group of students from his grade 12 class through the Purcell Mountains of British Columbia. Seventy kilometers in 6 days of hiking. Carrying everything we would need to survive a week in all sorts of weather we trudged through a wide variety of terrain: up mountains, down mountains; across streams and rivers on rocks, fallen logs and cable cars; through mud laden bogs and shoulder high scrub brush; scrambling under, over and on top of massive trees blown down by powerful winds – this was the most physically trying, testing and tortuous thing I have ever done in my life. On a number of occasions I was seriously wondering if I would be able to cover the distance we needed to cover in the time we had to cover it.

It seemed like every part of my body hurt – my shoulders, my hips, my back, my knees, I twisted my ankle numerous times, tendon pain would shoot up my right foot for no apparent reason. At one point when crossing a stream on two logs I leapt off onto a flat rock surface covered in an inch of water to discover is was as slick as a sheet of ice – I came crashing down on the rock with my 55 pound pack on top of me. I separated my shoulder, tore my rotator cuff, broke my finger and did some kind of damage to my elbow. However, there was no going back and no helicopter to magically fly me out of there. I had only one option – keep going.

I thought I had trained for this, but I was not prepared for the physical toll this trip would take on my body. Mental toughness was a strength I had to rely on more than anything. When my body was screaming out that I had to stop, my mind and heart had to keep me going. This was very tough for me.

The leader of the program who was my co-chaperone said that out of all the hiking he had done around the world this was the most difficult. We were testing out this hike for inclusion in the school's annual hiking trip for the grade 12s – it would not be added to the authorized routes. The school would never do this trip again. The only thing that seemed to keep me going was the fact that it would all be over in...4 days, then 3 days, then 2 days...

As I spent over 8 hours each day hiking while staring down at the person's feet in front of me on the trail, I would try to converse with the Lord about this experience. I realized that this hike was analogous to some of the life experiences that we have - experiences that many of you may be in the midst of right now.

These are difficult, arduous, demanding seasons of life that have you wondering how on earth you are going to survive. You are not sure if you have what it takes to work through this "dark night of the soul". Even as I tried to celebrate some of the many glorious aspects of this trip I found that, for the most part, what kept me going was knowing that it would all be over by Friday.

However, when we are in the midst of difficult seasons of life we do not know when they are going to end. Therefore, we must find our "song in the night". We must find the heart of God in the darkness of the difficulty. We must find Jesus' words of life in the pain of the process. Our "song in the night" enables us to have hope that we are not alone and the Lord will see us through.

If you are experiencing a dark night of the soul, or a demanding, difficult and arduous season of life I pray that you might find your "song in the night" from Jesus. He will not leave or forsake you. Cry out to Him in the midst of darkness and receive the comfort, hope and love He has for you.

A song in the night renews your strength to keep going in the midst of the darkness of difficulty. He is near you – draw near to Him.

Psalm 42:8
"By day the LORD directs His love, at night His song is with me - a prayer to the God of my life."

Psalm 77:6
"I remembered my songs in the night. My heart meditated…"

A TIME FOR ANGER

I just got back from my son's basketball game. The team they were playing was clearly a superior team. They had great skills, they were coached well, and they played hard. Bottom line: they were a great team. The final score was 110 to 35. What really got me angry was the fact that they full court pressed almost the entire game. In my books, that is just not good sports etiquette.

I used to do a lot of coaching. I've coached provincial champions, regional champions and zone champions in a few sports. One unwritten rule is that you don't run up the score and embarrass your opponent. Sure, play them hard, but don't crush them – especially in grade 10.

Our guys handled it really well. They were clearly frustrated and angry, but they maintained their composure. They played hard until the end. They channeled their anger. I tried to channel my anger too, but to be honest I was really pissed.

Here's my point – I haven't felt anger like that for a long time. Now, some of you guys out there may feel anger on a regular basis. I don't, and I think that's a problem. I believe that there is a time for anger. You see, anger is not a sin. What we do with it can be sinful. If anger is a sin, then God sins because scripture tells us He gets angry.

We need to get angry! Now please hear this – we don't need to get angry at petty little things. Unfortunately we tend to get angry at things we shouldn't, and don't get angry at things we should. Someone once said that a man is only as big as that which makes him angry. We need to get angry about things that really matter. We need to get angry with our own sin. We need to get angry with apathy. We need to get angry with injustice. We need to get angry with the enemy's strategy in our lives, in our marriages and in our children's lives. We need to get angry with the enemy's bullying!

Remember Popeye? "That's all I can stands and I can't stands no more!" Then he pounds the bad guy. How much crap are we going to put up with in our life and the lives of those we love before we get angry enough to do something about the enemy's strategy?

Our enemy is spiritual, the battle is real, and there is a time for anger. We must get angry with evil.

Ephesians 4:26
"Be angry and yet do not sin; do not let the sun go down on your anger."

A WONDERFUL LIFE

"If your heart is full of wonder you will live a wonderful life."

So here I stand at sunset on a secluded stretch of beach in Santa Barbara. I am waiting for the sun to set. It is beautiful, but it is taking a little longer than I thought. In fact, I am getting a little restless and impatient. Here I am amidst the wonders of God's glorious creation: rugged rock and vegetation strewn cliffs behind me; golden sands stretch out for miles to my left and right; the powerful Pacific Ocean crashes in wave after wave at my feet as the brilliant red flaming sphere we call the sun inches closer and closer to the horizon soon to give way to, and lend it's reflected glory to, the moon - while billions of other suns we call stars fill the night sky. And I am impatient because it's taking longer than I anticipated for the sun to set.

Isn't that pathetic?

What has happened to my heart? How have I lost the wonder and the mystery of it all? I have heard it said that "All over the world people are asleep, but the few who are awake live in a constant state of amazement." I don't want to be asleep – I want to live in a constant state of amazement. I want to be awake.

How about you? Do you feel asleep sometimes? Have you lost the wonder and the mystery of this life?

This simple sunset I am watching at the edge of the Pacific is full of mystery and wonder – God's glory. A few stats: The sun is 93,000,000 miles away from the earth. The light from the sun takes only 8 minutes to reach the earth. You could fit 1,000,000 earths into the sun. The sun is a flaming ball comprised primarily of hydrogen. As you know, the sun does not actually set. No, the earth is spinning at 1,000 miles per hour so that every 24 hours we make one complete revolution. We are spinning on an axis of 23.5 degrees. We are also flying through space at 67,000 miles per hour so that we rocket around the sun every 365 days. And, the gravitational pull of the sun keeps us in a precise orbit, while the earth's gravity keeps us all from flying off this planet we call home. Wow!

The Pacific Ocean is 65,000,000 square miles – 1/3 of the earth's surface - and almost 7 miles deep at its deepest point. It is filled with billions of organisms of all shapes and sizes. The vastness of it is beyond comprehension. In fact, we know more about the moon than we do about the ocean. The tides regularly come and go in response to the moon – how does that work??

Water evaporates from the ocean, in response to the sun, condenses on condensation nuclei to form clouds, which then rain down water on the earth to nourish life. This is the water cycle. Water molecules are continually being recycled. Does that mean that all the water that exists on the earth today is comprised of the same molecules that God spoke into being at creation?

And the air I am breathing as I watch this sunset is made possible by plants that absorb water and sunlight to produce oxygen through the miraculous compound known as chlorophyll. Amazing!

I am overwhelmed as I consider the mystery and wonder of what is going on around me to simply make my watching a sunset possible – not to mention the millions of mysteries that go on in my body to enable me to stand on the beach, see my surroundings, feel the wind, taste the salt air, hear the sea birds cry, and breathe oxygen to live...

God help me – help us - to choose not to live life asleep. Lord help us to be truly awake to the wonder, miracle and mystery of this life. May we choose to consider, explore, study, and investigate the mysteries of God all around us so that we might discover the glories of God and have hearts full of wonder, so that our lives might be wonderful.

Proverbs 25:2
"It is the glory of God to conceal a matter; to search out a matter is the glory of kings."

Isaiah 6:3
"...'Holy, holy is the Lord Almighty; the whole earth is full of His glory.'"

AIM FOR THE HEART, RAMÓN

A Fistful of Dollars - one of the original spaghetti westerns. Clint Eastwood versus the bad guys. In this case, Clint ends up in a deadly confrontation with the evil Ramón.

Ramón has one mantra: "If you want to kill a man, aim for the heart."

The movie culminates with a classic showdown. Ramón and his evil gang have terrorized the town and taken an old man captive – in order to lure Clint out. Suddenly, a huge explosion causes a massive cloud of dust to fill the air and obscure visibility. And, who should appear in the middle of the street, but the man himself. Poncho, six shooter, cigar.

"Let the old man go."

Ramón steps into the street and aims his lever action Winchester at Clint's heart. Boom. Clint falls down, but miraculously gets back up again. Again, boom. Time and time again Ramón pumps lead into Clint's heart, but Clint keeps on coming.

"Aim for the heart Ramón. If you're going to kill a man you have to aim for the heart."

The taunting infuriates Ramón. Finally after all Ramón's shots are spent, Clint reveals the iron plate he has strapped over his chest – with seven bullet indentations right over his heart. Ramón and his gang are then dealt with once and for all.

This is a great picture of the enemy's strategy for us – he goes after our hearts. He knows that if he's going to take you out, he has to take out your heart. If we lose heart we have lost everything. Your heart is the deepest part of you - your place of deepest conviction. The true essence of who you are. The life of God is found in your heart.

Guard your heart by strapping yourself with the truth. The truth of who God is. The truth of who you are. The truth of who your enemy is. Guard your heart by taking time to rest in the Lord. To listen. To drink in His love, His joy, His delight. Guard your heart by discovering God's heart and knowing His pleasure. Guard your heart by resisting your enemy and engaging in spiritual warfare. Fight back.

Your enemy aims for your heart – guard it.

Proverbs 4:23
"Above all else guard your heart, for it is the wellspring of life."

ALWAYS BE PREPARED

I had the pleasure recently of speaking with a young Canadian soldier who was heading off for a tour of duty to Afghanistan. He was a very well-spoken young man who seemed well prepared for his mission. At least, as well prepared as you can be prior to actually experiencing the chaos of war. He worked with the engineering corps. He will be part of large contingents of soldiers and equipment heading out into hostile territory. He will help identify and disarm IEDs (Improvised Explosive Devices). He will also be part of a tank section. He has been training for this deployment for three years.

He knew a great deal about the equipment that our troops will be using. Apparently the Canadians have some of the best equipment available. We utilize Leopard tanks - which are considered the best tanks in the world. Our other armoured personnel carriers are state of the art: the Coyote Reconnaissance Vehicle (CRV) and the Light Armoured Vehicle III (LAV III) – developed in Canada.

He spoke eloquently of the training and tactics that the Canadians utilize. There are actually large numbers of American troops that are under Canadian command in Afghanistan. This is a first – never before have American troops been under the command of another nation. The Canadians also fly American Mini Birds – given to us by the Americans - as well as our own Griffin helicopters with multiple chain guns. Yes, our Canadian troops are well trained and well regarded. We consistently prove ourselves to be an exceptional fighting force.

I was very impressed by this young man. He also helped me to become more aware of our troops, their training, their tactics and their effectiveness on the battle field. I was truly impressed and proud to be a Canadian. However, when I asked him one specific question his answer surprised me. I asked him why he's going over there – what is he fighting for? At first he said, "I don't know."

As I pressed the question he answered with a number of short statements, "I have been ordered to go. It's my duty. It's something our country is doing." I then asked him, "What is going to motivate you when the going gets tough?" He responded with, "The man next to me." So I asked, "What if the man next to you is questioning why he is there?" He said, "I don't know."

Aren't you fighting for the freedom of the Afghan people? Aren't you fighting to defeat a tyrannical oppressor of freedom? He indicated that he didn't really know. I was very surprised at his lack of understanding in regard to the reason behind his mission – Canada's mission. I encouraged him to work through this prior to his departure so he can articulate why he is fighting; so he can develop a conviction in regard to his mission.

I believe that we need to do the same. We need to know why we live the way we live. In II Corinthians 5 Paul gives us a glimpse into why he lived the way he lived. He knew that one day he would stand before Jesus to give an account for how he spent his life. He indicated that he is compelled by Christ's love to persuade others about Jesus.

Why do you live the way you live? We need to understand the reason for our mission. We need to be prepared to tell people why we have great hope. What motivates us? Why do we believe what we believe and do what we do? This is something we need to work through with Jesus in the context of His Word. I encourage you to wrestle through this.

Determine why you follow Jesus. Always be prepared to give the reason for your mission.

I Peter 3:15
"But in your hearts revere Christ as Lord. Always be prepared to give an answer to everyone who asks you to give the reason for the hope that you have. But do this with gentleness and respect,"

AN ATTITUDE OF GRATITUDE

For the most part, everybody likes a party. There are lots of different reasons to throw a party: birthdays, holidays, Christmas, Easter, retirements, Tupperware, engagements, etc. We really don't need a reason for a party, but it always helps to have a special occasion of some kind to provide us with the impetus to bring a group of people together to celebrate. Key ingredients for a successful party? People you like, food and beverage you like, music you like, mixed in with something special to celebrate and you've got all the fixins. These basic necessities make for a fairly decent get together.

There is a certain kind of party, however, that is never a good time. This party doesn't involve friends, food, beverages or music, but we seem to regularly join the party. In fact, I think that men in particular have a tendency to join this kind of party. Do you know the kind of party I'm talking about?

A pity party.

Yup, we all have a tendency to fall into self-pity and throw a little pity party. "My life is so hard. You don't understand the pressure I'm under. Nobody understands me. I don't have any real friends. My clients are such a pain. Money is so hard to come by. I never seem to have enough. I hate my car, but can't afford a new one. My staff is so self-centered. My kids are lazy. The beer is warm. The pretzels are stale. My steak is overcooked. My house is a black hole for repair bills. My boss is a jerk. God isn't coming through for me. God let me down...woe is me. Poor me."

My son would say, "Somebody call a waaaaaaaaambulance."

I am a pretty good pity partier. Hey, I can party with the best of them. I have a secret weapon though - my wife. Oh yes indeed, my wife can smell self-pity a mile away. She has absolutely no tolerance for self-pity – none whatsoever. She has given me a spiritual butt kicking on many occasions in an attempt to get me out of the party.

I've learned something else as well – it's the antidote to pity parties. This will help you never get sucked into a pity party again. This is the real secret weapon in your war against self-pity...

Thanksgiving.

Yes, an "attitude of gratitude" will help you steer clear of the pity party. As we choose to think about all those things we can be thankful for – in spite of whatever difficulties we may be experiencing – the mood of our heart shifts. As we offer thanksgiving to God the eyes of our hearts shift from ourselves to God: from our resources to His; from our weakness to His strength; from the lies of the enemy to the truth of God; from hopelessness to hope; from death to life. Thanksgiving is very powerful. Scripture tells us that a thankful heart actually prepares the way for us to receive the salvation of God.

Forget the pity party. Choose an attitude of gratitude – it's a way better party!

Psalm 50:23

"He who sacrifices thank offerings honors Me, and he prepares the way so that I may show him the salvation of God."

AN EPIC PERSPECTIVE

My son David has recently started his first year at university. He is at the beginning of a degree in International Relations. His ultimate objective – as he sees it at this point in his journey – is to help bring justice to oppressed Spanish-speaking people groups. He has a heart for justice and he loves the Spanish language and Hispanic culture. He wants to find out more about the Canadian Ministry of Foreign Affairs and see if that might be where the Lord is calling him to serve.

He is at that point in his life where the future is opening up wide. Through the international traveling we did during the two years that we home schooled the boys they discovered that the world is a very big place and that God, being a very big God, has a grand role for them to play in this epic adventure we call the Kingdom of God. David is very excited to be in a journey of discovery in regard to the place, the plan, the people and the purpose God has for him.

He wants to give of himself – his time, talent and treasure – to make a difference in this world. Yes, he finds himself spending countless hours working and studying hard in courses that seem to be totally irrelevant for what he ultimately wants to be doing. However, he understands that this is part of the process he must go through in order to ultimately do what he believes God is calling him into.

And so, in an attempt to keep his heart focused on the bigger picture, on the epic nature of the adventure into which he wants to walk with Jesus, David does something while he studies to call his heart up to a higher perspective. He has discovered a website called grooveshark.com. It's a music website where you can search any type of music and set up a playlist to listen to. David sets up his preferred music, straps on his headphones and listens to it while he works away at his seemingly insignificant first year studies. It's not the fact that he listens to music while he works that is so special. No, it's the type of music he is listening to...

He listens to the likes of Hans Zimmer, James Horner and Howard Shore. Who are these artists? They are some of the geniuses who compose the heart stirring scores to the movies that move us: Gladiator, Braveheart, Lord of the Rings, Blackhawk Down, Avatar, Crimson Tide, Pearl Harbour, Pirates of the Caribbean, Last of the Mohicans and others. David listens to these epic movie scores because he knows it stirs his heart and somehow keeps him engaged – at a heart level – in the belief that he is indeed created, crafted and called to play a significant role in the epic adventure called the Kingdom of God. He has landed on something here. I am listening to a collection of heart-stirring movie themes while I am writing this visional and I am being stirred.

Men, the reality is that our lives are more like Lord of the Rings than they are like Everybody Loves Raymond. We must do what we can every day to help keep the eyes of our hearts focused on and engaged in the bigger story – the epic adventure called the Kingdom of God into which we have been invited by the Risen Lord of Glory. Millions of beloved sons and daughters of our Heavenly

Father, "veterans of the faith", have gone before us carrying the torch of the testimony and are now cheering us on. Now is our time to carry the torch of the testimony high so that others might know all the life and love that their Heavenly Father has for them.

We are indeed created, crafted and called to play an irreplaceable role in this epic adventure. Let's do all we can to ensure we engage our hearts to maintain an Epic Perspective.

Hebrews, 12:1-3 (The Message)
"Do you see what this means—all these pioneers who blazed the way, all these veterans cheering us on? It means we'd better get on with it. Strip down, start running—and never quit! No extra spiritual fat, no parasitic sins. Keep your eyes on Jesus, who both began and finished this race we're in. Study how He did it. Because He never lost sight of where He was headed—that exhilarating finish in and with God—He could put up with anything along the way: Cross, shame, whatever. And now He's there, in the place of honor, right alongside God. When you find yourselves flagging in your faith, go over that story again, item by item, that long litany of hostility He plowed through. That will shoot adrenaline into your souls!"

AN OPEN HAND, NOT A CLOSED FIST

Do you watch American Idol? I can't stomach it. I know, everybody has a different opinion, but it's not for me. There are some very cool stories about the people who are auditioning and trying to "make it.", but the overall culture of the show is way over the top for me. I have never been able to watch an entire show. I caught parts of a gaudy spectacle this last week and had to turn it off.

A number of years ago when we were traveling in Britain we caught a few episodes of Britain's Got Talent – the show from which American Idol was fashioned. It's a totally different culture, though the essence of the show is the same. Average people audition hoping to be discovered. We were particularly moved by the story of Paul Potts, who eventually ended up winning the show. He was a shy, unassuming, slovenly phone salesman who was an amazing opera singer. It was marvelous to see his glory revealed.

However, what rubs me the wrong way is the way we seem to worship entertainers in North America. Singers, musicians, actors are all "idolized". Our culture is preoccupied with fame and fortune. A recent poll was conducted with thousands of young people who were asked to choose their preferred vocation from a list including: doctor, teacher, President of a well-respected university, politician, etc, including being an assistant to a famous person. The majority of them chose to be an assistant to a famous person. They didn't seem to care too much about shaping, leading and contributing to our society, they simply wanted to be around fame.

We seem to idolize fame. But I also think we idolize so much more. So, what is an idol? Idols are things we admire, adore and devote ourselves to. They are things we put our hope and trust in to give us life. Our culture is rife with idols. No, they are not the graven images of old that people would bow down to hoping to curry favour. No, our idols are far more sophisticated than that.

What do you look to for life? Where do you go for life that is outside of God? What do you put your hope and trust in apart from God? More money? A better job? A vacation you have been desperately wanting? Your business growing? More customers? Better customers? Healing? Alcohol? Your house? Your reputation? Your accomplishments? Your ministry? Your potential? Your glory? Your rights? Your health? Your car? Your boat? Your clothes? Sex?

Years ago the Lord helped me to catch a glimpse of the things that I desperately wanted to accomplish during my life so that I could consider myself a success. These were the idols in my life. The Lord then asked me to release all those things to Him. Idols are the things that we are afraid to offer up to the Lord because we couldn't stand the thought of losing them. You know something is an idol if you are afraid to give it to the Lord – if you are holding onto it too tightly. If you are willing for the Lord, for whatever reason, to take it from you, then it is not an idol for you.

We are called to hold onto the things the Lord gives us with an open hand, not a closed fist.

Ask the Lord to help you see what you are holding onto with a closed fist – it may very well be an idol for you. Our God is our everything, when we refuse to offer back to Him the very things that He has given to us we actually refuse the grace that He has for us to live by.

Carry all that God gives you with an open hand and receive all the grace He has for you.

Jonah 2:8
"Those who cling to worthless idols forfeit the grace that could be theirs."

ANCHORS OF TRUTH

Anyone who has done any boating knows that you need to be very aware of the weather before you depart on any outing. If you encounter any kind of hostile weather when you're out in a boat, you have only a few options: 1. Keep going and ride it out. 2. Find a safe harbour where you are protected from the storm and wait for it to pass. 3. Drop anchor, or tie up to a mooring buoy in a safer place and hold on.

Now, I'm no expert seaman by any stretch of the imagination, but I've experienced enough to know that a secure anchor is a critical lifeline in the midst of rough waters. We were "camping" once in a yacht on Okanagan Lake, tied up to a mooring buoy. At night the wind picked up, the lake got rough and if our anchor didn't hold we would have crashed onto the rocky shoreline. When storms whip up you have to know that the anchor you're tied to is going to withstand the pounding waves.

The same is true for the storms of life. In the midst of the storms that you're facing right now, what are the anchors of truth that you're holding onto? We cannot expect to sail through life without storms. They are a reality in this life and we've got to have anchors of truth to hold us secure in the midst of the storms. Here are a few anchors of truth that I cling to when I'm experiencing the storms of life:

Jesus won't give up on you!

Philippians 1:6 – "Being confident of this, that He who began a good work in you will carry it on to completion until the day of Christ Jesus."

You are deeply loved by God!

Romans 8:39 – "Neither height nor depth, nor anything else in all creation will be able to separate us from the love of God that is in Christ Jesus our Lord."

Jesus will take care of you!

Philippians 4:19 – "And my God will provide for all your needs according to His riches in glory in Christ Jesus."

God will show you the way!

Psalm 32:8 – "I will instruct you and teach you in the way you should go; I will counsel you and watch over you."

Jesus called you, you didn't call Him – He knows what He's doing.

John 15:16 – "You did not choose Me, but I chose you and appointed you to go and bear fruit – fruit that will last. Then the Father will give you whatever you ask in My name,"

He is bigger than anything you are facing!

Ephesians 3:20 – *"Now to Him who is able to do immeasurably more than all we ask or imagine, according His power that is at work in us."*

He knows the plan – you don't – and it's good!

Jeremiah 29:11 – *"For I know the plans I have for you,"* declares the LORD, *"plans to prosper you and not to harm you, plans to give you hope and a future."*

Choose to hang onto God's anchors of truth. They will hold you secure in the storms of life.

Psalm 27: 13, 14 *"I am still confident of this: I will see the goodness of the LORD in the land of the living. Wait for the LORD; be strong and take heart and wait for the LORD."*

ANGELS AMONG US

"Let's go kick his ass!"

These words sent a shock wave of fear through my friend's heart. He woke up to the reality that he had inadvertently wandered into the wrong neighborhood, at the wrong time, in a violent city. He now found himself alone on a dark street with nothing to protect him, nowhere to run, nowhere to hide and 3 men bearing down upon him with ill intentions.

My friend is a good man. He is a Godly man. He is a wholehearted follower of Jesus. He was in Los Angeles on business. His plane arrived around 9PM and once he arrived at his hotel he thought he would go for a little walk to get some air and find something to eat. He ambled along a fairly public stretch of road then turned to his left down a street that led to the ocean. As he took the corner he realized the street was very dark – no street lights. An intangible sense of foreboding began to wash over him.

The thought began to cross his mind that maybe he shouldn't be here. He had seen the group of 3 unsavory characters up at the top of the street as he turned to head down to the ocean. He now heard them put words to their intentions and saw them running down the street toward him.

Very little time to think; no time to act – and that's when it happened. What transpired next confounded him - he had never seen anything like this before...

The lead individual quickly bearing down upon him suddenly fell to the ground unconscious. His head appeared to be struck by an unseen force so violent it snapped his head back – he fell lifeless to the ground totally unconscious. The second individual close behind him, wielding a long skateboard as a weapon, fell beside his comrade, while his long board rocketed down the street toward the ocean. Two men now lay on the street – not of their own accord. The third man screeched to a stop while laughing hysterically at the predicament of his two friends.

"What just happened? Did I actually see that? Lord, was that an angel?" My friend wandered off in a state of spiritual bewilderment, wondering if indeed he had just witnessed an angel fighting on his behalf.

Scripture is filled with references to, and stories of angels. In fact, there are close to 300 references to angels in scripture. They are real and they are part of our everyday life. There is a spirit realm that is very real indeed. God commands His angels concerning us. They fight on our behalf against the demonic forces set against us, and they minister to us. When we pray, they take action. They realize the reality of our spiritual stature far more than we do. They know we are beloved sons of God, created in the image of God, filled with the Spirit of God, commissioned as ambassadors of God's kingdom to a world desperate for the redeeming power of God's love, and that we possess all authority in the name of Jesus.

As you read this e-visional there are angels with you. They see the spiritual stature you carry as a beloved son of God. They fight on your behalf on an ongoing basis, they minister to you and they respond to your prayers in the purposes of God. They know the power and authority you carry in the name of Jesus and long for you to walk fully in that.

Yes men, angels are among us – guarding, guiding, ministering and mighty in battle on your behalf. Thank you, Jesus. Help us to more clearly understand the nature of the spirit realm, the battle that rages, the role Your angels play in this epic adventure, and the role we play in impacting what goes on in heavenly realms.

Psalm 91:11
"For He will command his angels concerning you to guard you in all your ways;"

Hebrews 1:14
"Are not all angels ministering spirits sent to serve those who will inherit salvation?"

Hebrews 13:2
"Do not forget to show hospitality to strangers, for by so doing some people have shown hospitality to angels without knowing it."

ARE YOU AN IRONMAN?

We sat in a big semi-circle. Mostly young married couples, but couples of all ages. We had gathered in a hotel in downtown Winnipeg to spend the weekend at a marriage seminar. Unlike many men I had no reservations about being there. No, I was into this. I used to be quite involved in sports both as an athlete and as a coach, so I believed in the value of a coach. If I was willing to spend hours each day following the direction of a coach for a simple sport, then why wouldn't I be willing to receive some coaching for marriage.

So, there I sat next to my wife; ready to be coached in the greatest game ever. I was finding it a little difficult to engage so I soon found myself caught in a bit of a day dream. I looked down at my watch…

"You know, this is a great watch. Less than $40, it keeps good time, it's totally water proof, it has a stop watch, a timer, the date and it has a light. And, it just looks cool. I love the name too – Ironman."

It was then that the Lord seemed to whisper in my ear,

"That's what you think you are."

What? What was that? Was that you Lord? He began to help me unpack this thought: I thought I was an Ironman. I believed I had to be an Ironman. I didn't think I really needed anyone. You see, like most men I worshipped at the altar of the strong. I had to be strong. I had to be independent. I had to be self-sufficient. I couldn't show weakness. He then began to show me the impact that this was having on my marriage. My unwillingness to show any weakness was robbing Anne of intimacy. It was robbing us of intimacy.

When we refuse to admit our weakness we are really just posing. We all have weaknesses, but if we worship at the altar of the strong we are greatly intimidated by and, therefore, unwilling to show weakness. Our spouses feel like they are never really close to us because we always keep them at arm's length – "I can't show her any weakness." I was robbing Anne of intimacy because I was unwilling to show her any weakness. I needed to apologize to her for that and ask her for forgiveness. Not that I need to look to her for strength. No, I simply needed to be willing to be honest and then look to Jesus to be my strength.

Paul tells us that Christ's strength is manifest in our weakness. When we are weak, we can live in Christ's strength – only if we are willing to admit our weakness and ask the Lord to give us His strength.

Choose not to be an Ironman. Live in Christ's strength, not your own.

II Corinthians 12:9-10
"But He said to me, 'My grace is sufficient for you, for My power is made perfect in weakness.' Therefore I will boast all the more gladly about my weaknesses, so that Christ's power may rest on me. That is why, for Christ's sake, I delight in weaknesses, in insults, in hardships, in persecutions, in difficulties. For when I am weak, then I am strong."

ARE YOU HUNGRY AND THIRSTY?

We just returned from a fabulous weekend at one of our Band of Brothers Boot Camps. These are not physical boot camps; they are boot camps of the heart. We have been doing these boot camps for 8 years: this was somewhere around our 20th event. There were about 140 men who came to have God breathe life into the dry bones of their lives, come to life and stand up on their feet together as the army of God.

We have watched the Lord do miraculous works in the lives of men:

"My life was totally changed." "I was totally blown away." "This far exceeded my expectations." "My life was transformed this weekend." "The single most impactful spiritual experience I have ever had."

We continue to be in awe of how the Lord works powerfully in the hearts of men at these weekends. For years we have watched hundreds and hundreds of men marvellously transformed by the love of their Heavenly Father. We have also seen many men who for years have refused to come – for a wide variety of reasons. There have also been men who leave part way through the weekends and don't experience transformation. That is simply the reality of things. However, I find myself pondering why some men have profoundly powerful experiences while others do not.

Why is that?

I do not totally know why, but I have a hunch about something: I believe in order to experience more of what the Lord has for us we must be hungry and thirsty. We need to recognize we are broken and need healing. And, then we need to come to Jesus. Hungry and thirsty for more of Jesus, broken and know it, and choose to come to God. These are the prerequisites for new life.

Are you hungry and thirsty for life in Jesus, or have you fed yourself on religion or the things of this world? Do you see your need for healing, or are you "good"? Do you see Jesus as your only source of life, or do you go somewhere else for life?

I believe that this side of heaven we will always live in a state of divine dissatisfaction knowing a richness of true life in Jesus, but also knowing that there is so much more...

We cannot allow ourselves to be lulled into a state of complacency believing "this" is as good as it gets – that we can't expect anything better. We must always hunger and thirst for more of Jesus in us and through us.

I believe that every Godly man is marked by a hunger and thirst for more of Jesus. Not an empty, desperate, drivenness for something unattainable, but a desire for more of an immeasurable God who continues to touch our hearts and invite us deeper into his infinite love.

If you have lost your hunger and thirst for more of Jesus I would suggest you check your heart. Have you resigned yourself to this being as good as it gets, or have you filled your longings with something other than Jesus?

Oh Lord, help us to be men marked by a deep desire for more of You – more of Your Kingdom in us and through us. May we recognize the depth of our brokenness and the breadth of Your healing, and may we always choose to come to You because we know there is no life apart from You.

Hungry, thirsty and knowing Jesus is the only source of life. Then come to Him.

Isaiah 55:1
"Come all you who are thirsty, come to the waters and you have no money, come buy and eat! Come buy wine and milk without money and without cost. Why spend money on what is not bread and your labor on what does not satisfy?"

Matthew 5:6
"Blessed are those who hunger and thirst for righteousness, for they will be filled."

Jeremiah 2:13
"My people have committed two sins: They have forsaken Me, the spring of living water, and have dug their own cisterns, broken cisterns that cannot hold water."

ARE YOU LISTENING?

I heard it. Clear as day. Not loud. Not obvious, but it spoke to me.

I was walking along Kitsilano Beach in Vancouver. It was a spectacularly beautiful winter morning. A delicate layer of frost covered everything with a glistening sheen. The high tide waters of the Pacific were slack and unusually calm, like it lay sleeping. The brilliantly blue skies provided a marvelous back drop for the majestic mountains with their jagged peaks painted white with a dusting of snow. It was such a scene of glorious serenity that I wanted to do everything I could to be present and drink it all in.

I strolled along the path that mirrored the natural contours of the shore; bordered by beach and magnificently gnarled driftwood logs on one side and beautifully maintained grasses, trees and parks on the other. Park benches dotted the walking path providing ample opportunity for creation revelers to sit down, still themselves and drink in the grandeur of this Godly display of splendor. One particular bench beckoned me and I read the memorial plaque secured to it. This bench had been lovingly dedicated to a particular person who, I assume, loved to sit here, still themselves and drink in the grandeur. Their name was on the plaque with the words, "We're listening."

I heard it with my heart. It landed with some significance.

I then felt the Lord whisper, "Are you listening?"

Hmmm. I'm trying to. As best I know how I was trying on this gorgeous morning to listen. So what am I listening to? I want to hear God's heart expressed through the wonder of His creation. I want to hear whatever the Lord would say to me – a thought, a word, a song, an emotion, a memory, a vision, a hope, a dream, a fear, an experience... I want to nestle into God's perspective and that means I need to step out of many of the things cluttering my heart creating the din that crowds out the whisper of God.

In order to truly listen we need to be quiet. Now, that doesn't mean that we can't hear in the midst of noise or a cacophony of sound, but we hear far better when we are quiet. If we are talking with someone and truly want to hear them, we stop talking and listen, and if need be, we go somewhere that is quiet so we don't need to strain to hear them. Even if we are quiet it may still be difficult to truly listen to someone if we are distracted by issues running around our hearts and minds.

This is something I struggle with. I have so many ideas, thoughts, plans, musings, etc., running around my head that even though I am quiet and listening to someone I can still be distracted by what's rattling around in my mind. So, I have to choose to still myself – still my thoughts – and focus on the person at hand. This is called active listening. Actively engage. Actively still yourself. Actively listen.

I believe this is what the Lord has invited us to do on a regular basis – as a posture for living. We need to be actively listening to Him by stilling our hearts, calming our thoughts, surrendering our fears and anxieties and focusing on Him. Not "straining" to hear Him, but simply separating ourselves from the din of everyday life and saying, "Father would You please help me to hear Your heart – I am listening as best I know how. I want to hear You. What would You say to me?"

So men, the Lord is listening to your heart, are you choosing to still yourself and actively listen to Him? This is a practice we need to cultivate and become increasingly proficient at. In order to walk with Jesus we need to listen to Him.

Are you listening?

Matthew 17:5
"While He was still speaking, a bright cloud covered them, and a voice from the cloud said, 'This is my Son, whom I love; with Him I am well pleased. Listen to Him!'"

John 10:27
"My sheep listen to My voice; I know them, and they follow Me."

Psalm 81:13,14
"If my people would only listen to Me, if Israel would only follow My ways, how quickly I would subdue their enemies and turn My hand against their foes!"

Jeremiah 7:24

"But they did not listen or pay attention; instead, they followed the stubborn inclinations of their evil hearts. They went backward and not forward."

ARE YOU ON FIRE?

Outside the leaves had fallen, the mountain tops were frosted with snow and a winter chill was in the air. Inside my wife and I were sitting in the living room tucked into comfy chairs reading books with a crackling fire in the fireplace, and a little Van Morrison playing quietly in the background. What a great way to spend the late afternoon. We live in an older home with 2 wood burning fireplaces in the house; one in the living room and one in the man cave – I love our fireplaces.

There is just something fabulous about the snap, crackle and pop of the wood, the faint smell of smoke, the heat of the blaze and the red hot coals as the wood burns down to ash. Guys love fires, don't we? We can sit for ages around a fire just staring at it and poking it. Move the wood around a bit to get a bigger flame, throw some more wood on – we are fascinated by fire.

So, as we sat there by the fire and read, I would get up from time to time to poke the fire and put on more wood. I am box fire guy, not a teepee fire guy, but the secret to getting a good flame is to ensure the wood is close together with not too much space between the pieces of wood, but not too little either. I got up at one point when the fire had almost died out, yet there was still a lot of heat. There were two pieces of wood in the fire box, but they were a little far apart. So, I took out the poker and pushed the top piece a little closer to the bottom piece on a bit of an angle so they would overlap more. When I did that the wood burst into flame.

Wow, I wish I was like that. I wish I was "on fire" like that wood. Sometimes I feel like the wood that has a tiny little flame, is smoldering a bit, but not really on fire. Do you feel like that sometimes? Do you wish you were more on fire?

That phrase "on fire" was popular in the 70's; "Man, that guy is really on fire for Jesus!" It meant that someone was really passionate about following Jesus. He was always talking about Jesus and sharing with other people how much Jesus loves them, etc. I think it came from the 2nd chapter of Acts when the Holy Spirit fell on the disciples in "tongues of fire" and they were filled with the Holy Spirit.

Paul encourages us to "fan into flame the gift of God" in us. I take from this that we have a responsibility to cultivate our passion and the infilling of the Spirit of God. We can't just sit around passively, timidly asking the Lord to increase our passion for Him.

So, if we are not feeling "on fire" for Jesus what's wrong? I believe we can quench the Spirit's fire, and we can also simply get lazy, timid and passive.

How do we quench the Spirit's fire? We can do that through a variety of ways including cynicism, faithlessness, disobedience, disbelief and sin.

In regard to our responsibility to fan into flame God's gift in us, we must choose to draw near to God and the "fire" of the Spirit. We can choose to call out to him to fill us and reveal more of his heart and his will. We cannot be timid.

So, if you don't feel a burning passion for Jesus: Have you yielded yourself to Jesus? Have you come to Him with empty hands and an open heart? Have you fasted and prayed? Have you waited on Him in solitude and silence? Have you repented of sinful habits? Have you eliminated distractions? Have you read and studied? Have you engaged and chosen to serve others? Have you asked for more of His Spirit to fill you to overflowing?

Let's choose to draw near to Jesus to touch the flame of His Spirit, to set us on fire with passion for Him and His purposes in us and through us.

Are you on fire? If not, why not and what are you willing to do about it?

II Timothy 1:6
"For this reason I remind you to fan into flame the gift of God, which is in you through the laying on of my hands. For God did not give us a spirit of timidity, but a spirit of power, of love and of self-discipline."

I Thessalonians 5:19
"Do not put out the Spirit's fire; do not treat prophecies with contempt."

Acts 2: 3, 4
"They saw what seemed to be tongues of fire that separated and came to rest on each of them. All of them were filled with the Holy Spirit and began to speak in other tongues as the Spirit enabled them."

BACK COUNTRY

12 o'clock. 1 o'clock. 2 o'clock, 3, 4, 5 – every hour on the hour - until 7AM. I tossed and turned all night. Uncomfortable. Cold. Trapped in a tight space. Feeling very alone. Dreading every minute. Longing for the first rays of the dawn to bring hope of a new day – I was desperate for this night to end. It was -6 degrees and I was in a tent high in the Canadian Rockies. I was wearing long underwear with fleece pants, wool socks, a long sleeve turtle neck shirt, fleece jacket, wool toque and gloves. I was sleeping on a ½ inch mattress in a mummy bag zipped up over my head inside a 2-man tent. We were back country hiking and camping.

Backcountry is different from front country. You hike into the backcountry and, therefore, have to carry everything you need in your back pack. You want your pack as light as possible, so you take only the bare essentials. Some guys even cut their tooth brush in half to save weight. I am not that fanatical.

In front country camping you can typically drive right up to your campsite so you are not too concerned about weight. You take whatever you need to be comfortable and have a great holiday. We have probably all done some sort of camping. Some of you have probably perfected the art of camping – either backcountry or front country. I have never been that good at camping, but I do understand that backcountry is very different than front country...

So, here I am in the incredible splendor of the Canadian Rockies experiencing vistas and terrain that very few people in the world ever experience. Perhaps very few people are willing to pay the price to experience such terrain. But this night, this night was tortuous. It felt like all I did was hope for the morning to come. Now I know some of you guys are reading this and thinking – "What a wussy. C'mon man, you had all the right equipment." I know, I have no doubt that some of you have suffered through much more arduous conditions, but for whatever reason this night was brutal for me.

It then dawned on me that this night is a picture of how some of you men may be feeling about your lives. The Lord seems to have you in a very small place. You feel constricted and restricted with little room to move. This is a place of great discomfort with no quick way out. You feel cold and alone in the dark – not a lot of illumination. Your only hope is that the light of day will soon dawn with new opportunities, but for now you are trapped in the dark night of the soul hoping it will soon end.

The Lord led me into the spiritual backcountry a number of years ago and this was exactly how I felt. I believe that the Lord leads us into places like this, places where few men may be willing to go. This is a place to test the motivation of our hearts – will Jesus be enough? Will we be satisfied with Jesus, even when He feels very far away? Will we turn to Him to be our song in the night? Will we surrender our "right" to a comfortable and convenient life?

For millennia the Lord has led His men into the spiritual backcountry. Be encouraged to know that this is a journey others have taken before you. A new day will dawn, a new era of life, if you choose to surrender and embrace the Lord alone as your hope and song in the night.

Habakkuk 3:17-19

"Though the fig tree does not bud and there are no grapes on the vines, though the olive crop fails and the fields produce no food, though there are no sheep in the pen and no cattle in the stalls, yet I will rejoice in the LORD, I will be joyful in God my Savior. The Sovereign LORD is my strength; He makes my feet like the feet of a deer, He enables me to go on the heights."

BART WAS NOT A BLIND MAN

There he sat at the side of the road. Alone. Abandoned. Rejected. Reviled. Poor. Pitiful. Blind. Begging. Hopeless. Helpless.

Helpless? Maybe not...

Even though Bart was blind, he could see. He could see opportunity. And, his hearing was good. He heard a commotion – it sounded like a large group of people walking past where he was sitting. So, he grabbed someone and asked what's going on.

"Jesus is passing by."

Bart had heard the stories. He had heard that this Jesus was doing incredible miracles. He saw his opportunity and he took it. He started yelling at the top of his lungs, "Jesus, Son of David, have mercy on me!" Finally, Jesus heard him and told His disciples to bring the yelling man over.

"What do you want me to do for you?" Jesus asked him.

"I want to see." Bart said.

Jesus healed his blindness, and Bart followed Jesus.

We can learn a lot from Bart – a.k.a. Bartimaeus. Even though he was blind, he was not so blind as to miss his chance at freedom, healing and deliverance. He was not half-hearted in his pursuit of Jesus. He yelled at the top of his lungs. And, when people told him to sit down and shut up, he yelled even louder. He was desperate for Jesus.

You see, I think he understood that Jesus responds to faith. He knew that Jesus passes by us looking for faith, and if He doesn't find it, He passes us by. And, I think that his prayer is one of the most profound in scripture – "Jesus, Son of David, have mercy on me! I want to see!"

I pray this prayer regularly. Lord, have mercy on me and open my eyes to see the truth of who You are, Your heart toward me and this world, who You say I am and the role You have called me to play in this epic adventure...have mercy on me and open my eyes to see what I need to see – the things that I don't even know exist, because I can't see them. Open the eyes of my heart.

No, Bart wasn't totally blind. He saw his need for Jesus. He saw that he needed to passionately and wholeheartedly step out in faith and cry out for mercy to the One who has the power to save and to heal. He saw that he needed mercy. He saw that he needed healing. And, he saw that he was desperate to see.

We can learn a lot from Bart, because we're blind men too.

Mark 10:47-48

"...When he heard that it was Jesus of Nazareth, he began to shout, "Jesus, Son of David, have mercy on me...Many rebuked him and told him to be quiet, but he shouted all the more, Son of David have mercy on me..."

75

BE A LIGHTHOUSE

How do you say goodbye to your kids? How do you say goodbye to your wife?

"Have a nice day!" "Have a good day!" "Have a great day!" "See you later." "Stay safe." "Be good." "Live the adventure." "Go with God."...

How about "Be a lighthouse."?

I started saying that to my sons a while ago. I couldn't bring myself to say "Have a nice day." – "nice" is just such a nothing word. There is no passion or strength in "nice". "Have a good day" – better, but not enough of an exhortation. "Stay safe" – totally the wrong message. Jesus didn't call us to be "safe". Jesus isn't "safe", but He is good. "Live the adventure." - good, so I use that from time to time as well.

I somehow wanted to exhort my sons to catch a little glimpse of their calling each and every day. Now I know some of you are reading this and thinking, "Lighten up dude, it's just a goodbye." I know, I know, but I wanted my morning farewell as they went out into their worlds to perhaps bring some perspective to their interactions throughout the day.

It happens a little tongue-in-cheek now. When I say goodbye and I love you, they say, "Yeah, yeah I know – be a lighthouse"

Anne and I were recently on the Island of Kauai in the Hawaiian Islands and visited Kilauea Lighthouse. Built in 1913 at a cost of $78,000 it was quite an engineering and technological marvel. It stands 373 feet above the ocean and can be seen for over 26 nautical miles. The lens was shipped from France, weighs multiple tons and rotated on a simple axis of a bowl within a bowl filled with liquid mercury. There was no electricity in 1913 so the light that shone for 26 miles was from a kerosene lantern. It is no longer operational, having been replaced by a simple solar powered rotating beacon, but remains one of the most visited attractions in the Hawaiian Islands.

So what is the function of a lighthouse? Well, as best as I can understand it, they are a warning and a welcome for mariners: a warning that land is here so be careful not to run aground and sink your ship; a welcome that land is here so you can find some safe harbour.

I am sure that if you are in a ship at sea on a long voyage you want to make sure you are aware of any potentially hazardous land that could end your grand adventure by destroying your boat – and perhaps your life. In addition, if you have been lost at sea and buffeted by storms that threaten to sink your ship and perhaps destroy your life, then you would be very pleased to see the light of a lighthouse to indicate that land is near and, hopefully, a safe harbour.

Jesus told us that we are to be light to the world, and not to be bashful about it, but let it shine so that people can see our good works and glorify God. Don't hide your light under a basket – let it shine. We need to help people recognize the safe harbour they can find in Jesus. We also need to help them recognize the dangerous rocks in life that can destroy them.

So how do we do that? Well, I think that is a good thing to ask Jesus about. "Lord, how can I be a light to people in my life today?" "How can I help this person I am interacting with to see a little more clearly the safe harbour - the life - that you have for them? Is there also some way that I can help them become more aware of the destructive rocks and reefs that the enemy would shipwreck them upon."

Let's ask the Lord to help us to be lighthouses for Him – to help illuminate for others the life He has for them and the destruction the enemy intends. Don't be bashful – let your light shine.

Be a lighthouse.

Matthew 5:14-16
"You are the light of the world. A town built on a hill cannot be hidden. Neither do people light a lamp and put it under a bowl. Instead they put it on its stand, and it gives light to everyone in the house. In the same way, let your light shine before others, that they may see your good deeds and glorify your Father in heaven."

BE BOLD!

My son and I just returned from a trip to Ottawa – our nation's capital.

I needed to fly to Ottawa for business and David was on a reading break at university from his studies in International Relations. At this stage in his "vocational vision quest" he wants to be part of an international agency bringing justice to impoverished people groups around the world. So I thought it might be cool if he came with me and we set up some meetings with a number of relevant agencies in Ottawa.

After many web searches, phone calls and emails I managed to set up a number of very interesting meetings. Over the course of two days I secured meetings with the United Nations Association of Canada, the United Nations High Commission for Refugees, the Executive Assistant of a Federal Cabinet Minister, the Director of the Conservative Party Youth Internship Program, as well as an invitation to attend a special evening for refugee issues at the University of Ottawa sponsored by the UNHCR. However, we got refused by one particular agency.

The Canadian Department of Foreign Affairs (DEFAIT) refused to grant us a meeting. The email response I got – after numerous phone calls and emails – indicated that they do not meet with the general public on these types of issues, but directed me to their website where more information was available. The email was from a Deputy Director.

Dang - I was a little disappointed by this response. This is my son we are talking about and Foreign Affairs is the big kahuna. However, I now had a response from someone on the inside, and half the battle of breaking through the bureaucracy is actually getting to a person on the inside who has some authority. I had now found my person.

So, I pushed back. I wrote back and respectfully asked if she could make an exception for my son. I suggested that she could probably empathize with a young person wanting to find out more about their potential vocation – especially a vocation as wide ranging and convoluted as International Relations. I told her about the other meetings we had secured (to create positive peer pressure), and I informed her about my son's accomplishments (humanitarian awards, foreign service, etc.) in an attempt to demonstrate that my son is indeed serious about and committed to making a positive global contribution through his chosen field of endeavor.

She replied that she would be pleased to meet with us. Fabulous.

Thank you Lord and thank you to the people who agreed to meet with us. I was pumped that in the course of 7 days the Lord had opened up some very cool doors for us in Ottawa. However, these doors would not have opened if I had not been bold.

Now, I don't tell you this story to say, "Hey, look at me and be bold like me." Man, I battle timidity and passivity regularly. This situation has simply served to remind me that we are encouraged throughout scripture to be bold. And, when we are bold the Lord opens doors.

Boldness is a choice. It is a choice to not give in to fear, faithlessness, insecurity, intimidation, passivity, and mediocrity – those things that keep us from attempting the extraordinary and walking wholeheartedly with Jesus. Boldness is a decision to deal ruthlessly with sin in our lives as well, because sin robs us of God-given boldness. "The *righteous* are as bold as a lion."

Boldness also comes from the Holy Spirit. Read the book of Acts. When the early believers were filled with the Holy Spirit, boldness was always one of the key manifestations.

I believe that if we are to truly apprehend that for which the Lord has apprehended us, we must be bold. Let's believe the truth of who God is and who He says we are. Let's deal with the sin in our lives and continually ask the Lord to fill us with the Holy Spirit.

Let's be bold!! Ask, seek, knock and I am sure we'll be surprised the doors that the Lord opens.

Luke 11:8-10

"..I tell you, even though he will not get up and give you the bread because of friendship, yet because of your shameless audacity he will surely get up and give you as much as you need. So I say to you: Ask and it will be given to you; seek and you will find; knock and the door will be opened to you. For everyone who asks receives; the

one who seeks finds; and to the one who knocks, the door will be opened.

Proverbs 28:1
"The wicked flee though no one pursues, but the righteous are as bold as a lion."

Hebrews 4:16
"Let us therefore come boldly unto the throne of grace that we may obtain mercy, and find grace to help in time of need."

BE STRONG. BE COURAGEOUS.

There I sat in the cab of the 1 ton dump truck waiting for who-knows-what to arrive and fill my order. This was the first time I was at an aggregate supply yard. I was 19 years old, and very intimidated. I had been sent by the owner of the landscape company I worked for between university terms to pick up 2 cubic yards of 1.5 inch drain rock. I knew what the drain rock looked like, but I had no idea how much 2 cubic yards was and I really didn't know what was involved in getting it into my truck.

As I sat there intimidated by these unknowns and by the mountains of material that surrounded my truck I felt something that did nothing to calm my insecurities. The ground began to rumble around me – something akin to minor earth tremors – followed by a deafening roar that sounded like a jet engine. My eyes then beheld the largest piece of motorized equipment I had ever seen in my life – an 8 cubic yard front-end loader. Now, I know for many of you guys that may be a little girlie loader, but for a 19 year old North Vancouver middle class city slicker it was gigantic.

The big, burly, hairy driver opened the door and yelled something intimating at me, which I interpreted as meaning, "What do you want and how much of it do you want?" I pointed at the mountain of drain rock and held up 2 fingers. He yelled back what I think was, "Tell me when to stop." He then partially filled his bucket, rumbled over to my truck and gingerly shook out some drain rock. I timidly told him to stop – having no idea how much 2 yards looked like and no idea if I even had what I came here for. He left abruptly.

I drove back to the weigh scale on the way out to talk with the same rough, burly, intimidating guy I timidly asked on the way in how I get 2 yards of 1.5 inch drain rock. He was the one who told me to drive over to the mountains of rock and wait. When I reached the scale on the way out he said, "I thought you wanted 2 yards of drain rock?"

"Ah, yeah I do, but don't really know how much that is and the guy in the massive loader seemed to be in a hurry."

Then the God moment arrived – my significant life lesson began...

The rough, burly, intimidating guy looked me square in the eyes and said boldly and matter-of-factly as only a manly man could, "Look kid, you came here to get 2 yards of 1.5 inch drain rock. Don't leave until you have it!" I am sure there were some colorful expletives mixed in there for good measure, but the underlying sentiment was clear, "Man up kid." Or to put it in the Biblical vernacular, "Be strong and courageous!"

So, emboldened with a newfound confidence, and knowing that I only had 1 yard of drain rock, I drove back to mountains of rock and then boldly took charge of commanding the guy in the massive loader to give me one more yard. Which he did, and I left a changed man.

My lesson was very simple: sometimes we just need to man up. We need to choose to be bold and courageous. Cowboy up. Nut up or shut up. However you want to put it, we simply need to choose to be strong. It's part of being a man.

So, you may very well be facing some very intimidating scenarios right now. Yes, get prayer. Yes, seek wisdom from the Lord. Yes, surrender to His will and ask for strength. Then, man up. Be strong, be courageous – they are both choices. Follow in Joshua's footsteps.

Be strong. Be courageous. Be a man.

Joshua 1:9

"Haven't I commanded you? Strength! Courage! Don't be timid; don't get discouraged. GOD, your God, is with you every step you take." (The Message)

BEER WITH JESUS

My son Benjamin came home from work and said he heard an awesome song on the radio about "If I could have a beer with Jesus". We Googled it and had a listen. Wow. This song has such an honest, raw and tender emotion to it about a man who would love to sit down and have a beer with Jesus to talk about the stuff of life. No religious overtones, no super-spirituality – just a man who has a tender heart for Jesus and is thirsty for time with his Lord.

"If I could have a beer with Jesus,
heaven knows I'd sip it nice and slow.
I'd try to pick a place that ain't too crowded,
or gladly go wherever he wants to go.
You can bet I'd order up a couple tall ones,
tell the waitress put 'em on my tab.
I'd be sure to let him do the talkin' –
careful when I got the chance to ask...

How'd you turn the other cheek to save a sorry soul like me?
Do you hear the prayers I send?
What happens when life ends?
And when you think you're comin' back again?
I'd tell everyone, but no one would believe it –
if I could have a beer with Jesus.

If I could have a beer with Jesus,
I'd put my whole paycheck in that jukebox.
Fill it up with nothing but the good stuff;
sit somewhere we couldn't see a clock.

Ask him how'd you turn the other cheek
to save a sorry soul like me?
Have you been there from the start?
How'd you change a sinner's heart?
And is heaven really just beyond the stars?
I'd tell everyone, but no one would believe it –
if I could have a beer with Jesus.

He can probably only stay for just a couple rounds,
but I hope and pray he's stayin' till we shut the whole
place down.

Ask him how'd you turn the other cheek
to save a sorry soul like me?
What's on the other side?
Is mom and daddy alright?
And if it ain't no trouble tell them I said "hi".
I'd tell everyone but no one would believe it –
if I could have a beer with Jesus."

As I listened to the song I found myself longing for the opportunity to do just that – sit down all alone with Jesus and talk.

Then the thought hit me – what's stopping me?

I think Jesus asks me regularly to sit down with Him with the beverage of my choice – a glass of wine, a caramel macchiato, a chocolate martini, a water, a beer – whatever. Sadly though, I am often too busy with other things to sit down alone with Him and commune.

Rick

The fact is, Jesus is alive. Jesus has promised He is with us and will never leave us or forsake us. Sure, it would be awesome if we could see Him face to face and talk. Not yet for the face to face; but nothing is stopping us from communing with Him now except our own choice not to. We can invite Him into every aspect of our lives. And, we can choose to steal away with Him anytime – He has given us an open invitation.

Let's take him up on it. Beer with Jesus. Wine with Jesus. Walk with Jesus. Bible study with Jesus. Hike with Jesus. Alone on the beach with Jesus. Boat with Jesus. Silence and solitude with Jesus. You fill in the blank - _____ with Jesus.

May this song help to awaken a deep inner thirst in you for more of Jesus. And then, take Him up on His open invitation. Let's do EVERYTHING with Jesus.

Matthew 28:20

"…And surely I am with you always, to the very end of the age."

Acts 1:3

"After his suffering, He showed himself to these men and gave many convincing proofs that He was alive. He appeared to them over a period of forty days and spoke about the Kingdom of God."

John 14:18-19

"I will not leave you as orphans; I will come to you. Before long, the world will not see me anymore, but you will see Me. Because I live, you also will live."

Hebrews 13:5

"Keep your lives free from the love of money and be content with what you have, because God has said, 'Never will I leave you; never will I forsake you.'"

BELOW SEA LEVEL

As I started this year I became aware of a heaviness that I was feeling. I really couldn't pinpoint anything in particular that would have led to these feelings, but the feelings were all too familiar to me: discouragement, hopelessness, despair.

C'mon – I can't believe that I'm feeling this again. How often do I have to deal with this? Like most stoic men I gutted it out for a few days trying not to pay attention to my feelings. I simply tried to get on with things, trusting that the feelings would soon pass. However, the feelings didn't pass. As I took a little time to actually talk about this with the Lord, He helped me remember that these feelings have dogged me, at various times and for various durations, for years. That's right, I remember now, this is part of the ongoing strategy of the enemy set against me. So, I began to rebuke the strategy of the enemy and, lo and behold, my emotions shifted. Gone were the feelings of discouragement, hopelessness and despair.

Why do I have to keep fighting against this? Why does this keep coming back to haunt me? Why do I forget how to deal with this, suffer through it for a while and then remember that this is an ongoing strategy of the enemy? Frankly, I don't know. I actually got impatient about always having to struggle with this kind of thing in my life. I got ticked off about it. So, I asked the Lord if He could give me a picture that would give me some perspective. He did, and what He showed me I found extremely helpful...

The Lord brought to mind Holland. Holland is a very unique country because most of it is below sea level – two thirds in fact. For hundreds of years, the Dutch have diligently worked to keep the North Sea, and numerous rivers, at bay so that their land will not be flooded by the relentless tides set against them. Using an ingenious system of dikes, dams, levies, flood ways, gates, drainage ditches, canals, breakwaters and pumping stations (think iconic windmills) the Dutch have fought against the sea, and won.

If the Dutch are not diligent about resisting the sea on an ongoing basis, as well as preparing for normal and unprecedented storm surges, they will lose the ground that they have so diligently fought for. So, over the course of hundreds of years the Dutch have continued to initiate and integrate ingenious means to fight against the tides, and for the lifestyle they have created in the Netherlands. Complacency will lead to disaster and their demise.

Diligence = life. Complacency = death. Diligence = victory. Complacency = defeat. Diligence = overcome. Complacency = overwhelmed.

The Dutch realize that, due to the reality that they live below sea level, they must be diligent to prepare for and fight against rising waters. Their current system is built to withstand a 10,000 year storm. However, they know that complacency will be their downfall, so they are continually testing and strengthening their defenses.

We are like the Dutch – we live below sea level spiritually. The enemy who opposes us is defeated, but he is not destroyed. So, we must be diligent to utilize all the means Jesus has equipped us with to keep the tide of the enemy's strategy at bay. Our diligence leads to life – complacency leads to destruction.

So, what has Jesus equipped us with to stem the demonic tide set against us? Prayer, worship, praise, scripture, humility, spiritual warfare, repentance, tithing, generosity, fellowship, kindness, service, grace, mercy – are just a handful of the myriad means Jesus has equipped us with to keep the enemy at bay and live in the freedom of the Government of God in us and through us.

This side of heaven we live below sea level and must be diligent to continually resist demonic tides of oppression. Our diligence will lead to life, but our complacency will lead to our destruction.

Proverbs 1:32, 33
"For the waywardness of the simple will kill them, and the complacency of fools will destroy them; but whoever listens to me will live in safety and be at ease, without fear of harm."

I Peter 5:8, 9
"Be alert and of sober mind. Your enemy the devil prowls around like a roaring lion looking for someone to devour. Resist him, standing firm in the faith, because you know that the family of believers throughout the world is undergoing the same kind of sufferings."

BILBO'S EPIC ADVENTURE

"I am looking for someone to share in an adventure that I am arranging, and it's very difficult to find anyone."

"I should think so - in these parts! We are plain quiet folk and have no use for adventures. Nasty disturbing uncomfortable things! Make you late for dinner! I can't think of what anyone sees in them."

And so Bilbo Baggins resists Gandalf's invitation to join him in an epic adventure.

As I began rereading The Hobbit in anticipation of the release of the movie, I empathized with Bilbo to a certain degree. Jesus is calling us into a grand adventure. An adventure full of life, but full of risk as well. For if a journey has no risk it is not an adventure. Risk is the very essence of adventure. Risk demands faith – and our journey is one of faith.

Bilbo resisted Gandalf's invitation because he wanted a safe, comfortable existence, one where he was never late for dinner. Everything is provided and nothing is demanded of him that is not too arduous; and he most certainly is not forced into anything for which he feels unprepared and ill equipped.

Does that sound familiar? I wish life were like that sometimes – don't you?

In The Hobbit, Gandalf does not take no for an answer and Bilbo finds himself in an adventure that firmly and decisively places him well outside his comfort zone. In the early discussions about the adventure in the midst of his fear and insecurity, as he listens to the stories and songs of the true adventurers with whom he is journeying (the Dwarves), he experiences a brief epiphany...

"Then something Tookish woke up inside him, and he wanted to go and see the great mountains, and hear the pine trees and the waterfalls, and explore the caves, and wear a sword instead of a walking stick."

And so, with no small degree of reticence, Bilbo reluctantly joins the epic adventure that would ultimately forge him into the famous Hobbit he became.

In the midst of his insecurities and the hesitation his companions have about whether Bilbo has what it takes for this adventure, Gandalf exclaims,

"I have chosen Mr. Baggins and that ought to be enough for all of you...there is a lot more in him than you guess, and a deal more than he has any idea of himself."

As I read this piece of classic literature I couldn't help but be impacted by how this story so closely reflects our epic adventure of journeying with Jesus. Our journey is filled with excitement, fear, insecurity, joy, hopelessness, hope, danger, injury, triumph and tragedy, and much, much more. Yes, this is what I long for...no, I don't want this. I will follow You forever...stop, I've had enough.

What keeps us committed to this journey?

Well, like Bilbo I believe it is two things: knowing we are called, and the community with whom we are journeying. I think we know that our lives as partners with Jesus in the epic adventure of the Kingdom of God will not always be "...pony rides in May sunshine...", but knowing that He has called us, loves us, will never leave us or forsake us and that nothing can separate us from His love keeps us plodding on. In addition, we need co-journeyers to remind us of this Truth and encourage us when we lose vision, hope or heart.

A few questions for you:

Have you said yes to Jesus' invitation to step out of your comfort zone into a glory that He knows you have, but you do not? Or, have you chosen comfort, convenience, safety and solitude?

If you have said yes to the Call, are you walking closely with the Caller reminding yourself of the Truth amidst the difficulty? Or, have you wondered off alone?

Have you chosen to commit to a community of fellow journeyers who can help remind you of the Truth when you lose vision, hope and heart? (And do the same for them.) Or, have you wondered off alone from the community?

Jesus sees a glory and strength in us that we do not see in ourselves. Let's wholeheartedly join together with Him in the epic adventure of the Kingdom that we might not be the same - and have a tale or two to tell...

John 12:26

"Whoever serves Me must follow Me; and where I am, My servant also will be. My Father will honor the one who serves Me."

Romans 8:38, 39

"For I am convinced that neither death nor life, neither angels nor demons, neither the present nor the future, nor any powers, neither height nor depth, nor anything else in all creation, will be able to separate us from the love of God that is in Christ Jesus our Lord."

Hebrews 11:6

"And without faith it is impossible to please God, because anyone who comes to Him must believe that He exists and that He rewards those who earnestly seek Him."

BLESSED WITH A BURDEN

My wife teaches teachers at a university. For close to 30 years she has been passionate about teaching. She currently works with teachers-in- training – she loves it. She has a burden to help student teachers become the best teachers they can be.

In light of my wife's passion for teaching, we have watched a number of movies about teachers and teaching over the years. One of the movies we have watched a number of times is called "Freedom Writers". It's the true story of teacher Erin Gruwell who passionately and tirelessly worked with "throw away" teens in an inner city school to help them achieve far more than they – or anyone else in their lives – ever thought they could. Her unorthodox tactics and techniques put her at odds with some in the system, but the change she facilitated in the lives of her students won her critical acclaim through the best-selling book "The Freedom Writers Diary".

At one point in the movie she is at dinner with her upper middle class father who can't really understand why his highly educated daughter with the world at her doorstep is so passionate about working in an impoverished school with delinquent youth. After listening to her enthusiastically describe what her work entails and how much she loves working with these teens – even in the midst of the pressures, stresses and opposition – he said something to her that has stuck with me ever since: "You have been blessed with a burden."

Wow. Blessed with a burden. What burden am I blessed with?

A burden is different than a passion. A passion can be selfish – it does not need to be about the well-being of others. A burden however, is about others. It involves sacrifice. It is costly in some measure. It can be inconvenient and uncomfortable, but you are compelled to do it. You are compelled to give of yourself for the benefit of others. In some respects you cannot stop yourself from engaging.

There are two kinds of motivation: intrinsic and extrinsic. Intrinsic comes from within. Extrinsic comes from outside. More money, pleasure, comfort, position, advancement, promotion, etc. – these are all extrinsic motivators. In many ways we are extrinsically motivated. Intrinsic motivation, however, is something that resides within you. Some refer to it as "fire in your belly". A burden is definitely intrinsically motivated. Sure, there may be some extrinsic benefits, but even if there weren't any you would still press on.

I have often, throughout the years, admired my wife's undaunted focus on education and teaching. I have looked at my wide and varied career path and questioned why I wasn't more like my wife. Do you ever do that? Do you compare yourself to others who seem so motivated and so focused and ask why you can't be more like that? (And then typically get a little bummed out about it.) We can't do that, men. We must walk wholeheartedly with Jesus on the path He is leading us, even if it may seem like a detour sometimes.

I think that the Lord's burden we end up carrying does not suddenly fall on us out of the heavens. I think the burden grows as we begin to engage in a need. As we begin to step out of ourselves to somehow, some way give to others we begin to acquire the burden the Lord has for us. Oh, I know that He wants to impart His heart – His burden – to us, but we must first surrender and obey. Surrender our hearts to Him, and then step out in obedience to meet a need. It's in the place of laying our lives down for the benefit of others that we discover the Lord's heart and begin to acquire the burden that He has for us to carry. We become compelled by His love.

We can all be blessed with a burden as we seek God's heart, surrender our will to Him and then step out in obedience to serve others. And, what a blessing the burden can be.

I Corinthians 9:16
"For when I preach the gospel, I cannot boast, since I am compelled to preach. Woe to me if I do not preach the gospel!"

Bring Your Lunch

I was sitting in a coffee shop just about to start writing in my journal and try to connect with the Lord. To tell you the truth, I was bummed out. I wasn't really hearing the Lord very well. I was tired and weary, visionless, faithless – my viz was not good. Anyways, a guy comes in who has been to our Boot Camp and sits down to talk with me. He begins to share where he is at, and it's not a dissimilar place to mine.

We are sharing back and forth some of our challenges and finding some common ground. He then states that he really wants to be mentored so that he can mentor others, because he doesn't feel that he has much to offer others right now. When he shares this something goes off in my spirit – a little red flag pops up and I think, "I don't know if I agree with that." You see, this man is a father of adult children. This man loves Jesus and faithfully walks with Him as best as he knows how. This man is gifted and has shared his gifts with me in the past in ways that have helped me with what the Lord has been leading me into. This man is an active and engaged member of a vibrant church. This man has a lot to give. This man has the Spirit of the Living God alive in him.

So, I tell him that I don't agree with him. Yes, pursue a mentor. Ask the Lord to bring someone into your life who can further disciple you. However, you have a lot to give right now. I think of the story of the feeding of the five thousand...

Remember when Jesus fed the 5,000? Amazing – yes? A great miracle by any account, but how did it start? A key player in this incredible event was a young boy. The kid who brought his lunch made all the difference. Three key lessons we can learn from that boy: 1. Show up. 2. Bring your lunch. 3. Share your lunch.

You see, first of all the kid showed up. He wasn't hiding. He didn't stay home. He just showed up – he chose to be there, to be present.

Then he chose to bring his lunch. He brought some resources. He brought what he had. It was a humble lunch, but he brought it.

Lastly, he gave it away. He figured that the Lord could do more with it than he could. He offered what he had to the Lord and to others.

That's exactly what the Lord is asking us to do: Show up. Bring what we have and then give it away. All of us can do that. You'll be amazed what the Lord will do.

John 6:9
"Here is a boy with five small barley loaves and two small fish, but how far will they go among so many?"

BULL'S-EYE THEOLOGY

Have you had much experience with targets? I am sure that we all have a working knowledge of how targets typically work. The target has a center point that you are trying to hit – it's called the bull's-eye. There are various rings surrounding the bull's-eye, but the center of the target is what you are aiming for.

Ever play with bows and arrows as a kid? Do you remember your first bow? Did you make it, or was it store bought? The problem with arrows was that it was hard to find a target they could stick into and not cause damage. I remember going to summer camp as a young boy and being introduced to serious archery. Great big straw backed targets with a big bull's-eye to try and hit. What was so cool about this was the fact that the arrow would actually stick into the target and not just ricochet off and impale my friends.

BB and pellet guns anyone? Cardboard boxes were great for target practice. Take a felt pen, draw a target on the front of the box then go for it. It was easy to see how your shots were grouped and how close you came to the bull's-eye. You could also measure how good you were compared to your friends. In fact, that's how marksmanship is measured – how well you cluster your shots as close as possible to the bull's-eye.

I once got a little too creative with my target practice as a boy. I found my older brother's BB gun downstairs in the storage room. Upon further exploration I found a box of Christmas tree ornaments.

Hey, what could be better that actually having a target that explodes? I had the time of my life setting up all those lovely breakable ornaments and then blasting them to smithereens. Well, at least until my dad found out...but I digress. The point is we have all had the concept of targets and bull's-eyes firmly planted into our psyches. The goal is to get as close as possible to the bull's-eye and not deviate away from it – if you do you are missing the mark.

I think we tend to view the will of God as a bull's-eye – we are either hitting it or missing it. We can live in this pressure to be precisely hitting the mark with God and not to deviate. We see the will of God as being very narrow and live with an overriding fear that we are not really in His will, and therefore, falling short. We tend to judge ourselves as regularly falling short. We live with an overriding sense of defeat, feeling that 'I am not good enough.'

I used to believe this. I now see things differently.

Jesus told a parable of the talents where the master gave each servant various talents according to each individual's ability. He then said that he wanted to see a return and left them to it. He didn't tell them what to do or how to do it; he simply wanted a return on his investment. Now, he had spent time with them so they knew him and understood his heart. He was asking them to steward his property. However, there was a large degree of freedom each one had to create a return on the master's investment.

I believe that this is what God's heart is toward us. He entrusts to us various talents, abilities, resources and desires. He has provided us a glimpse into His heart through scripture and the Holy Spirit and asks us to faithfully invest what He has entrusted to us to create a return for His Kingdom. He is looking to see if you believe and trust in Him and have faithfully invested what He has given you to create a return.

Do not bury your talent because you think you don't have what it takes to hit the bull's-eye, that somehow you will miss the mark. God's will is bigger than you think and His heart for you is good. Go for it. God's will is not a bull's-eye.

Matthew 25:14-30
"Again, it will be like a man going on a journey who called his servants and entrusted his wealth to them. To one he gave five bags of gold, to another two bags, and to another one bag, each according to his ability. Then he went on his journey. The man who had received five bags of gold went at once and put his money to work and gained five bags more. So also, the one with two bags of gold gained two more. But the man who had received one bag went off, dug a hole in the ground and hid his master's money..."

BULLY BEATDOWN

My sons and I discovered a new show online: "Bully Beatdown." (Now, I know there are internet rumors that this show is not exactly what it claims to be, but it is still very compelling.) The concept of the show is simple: a bully gets invited to spend two rounds in the cage with a Mixed Martial Arts (MMA) fighter for the chance to win $10,000. Adult men who are being bullied send a video into the host of the show – a successful MMA fighter in his own right. The videos describe what this particular bully has been doing in the lives of the applicants to warrant a "beatdown". The successful applicant then gets visited by the host with a camera crew to confront and challenge the bully.

If the bully accepts the challenge he is provided with some degree of MMA training in preparation for the beatdown. The bully will start each round with $5,000. In the first "submission" round he will lose $1,000 every time he taps out from an arm bar, leg bar or choke hold, with that money being given to his victim. In the second "striking" round he will lose all $5,000 if he gets knocked out, suffers a technical knockout, or the ref has to stop the fight – with the funds being given to his victim. The cage fight takes place in front of an audience who are all clearly disgusted with the bully and regularly chant "beatdown, beatdown, beatdown". Everyone wants to see the bully get his due.

Enter the MMA fighter. A champion within the MMA world. Deadly. Dangerous. And intent on teaching this bully a lesson. Fully committed to giving him a beatdown. The champion doesn't make any claims that he can't back up. He does not make idle threats. No, he has the power to do exactly what he intends to and exactly what the great crowd of witnesses has come to see. The thirst for justice is palpable. We have shared in the tragic story of the victim and now want justice to be served. However, the bully remains arrogant and defiant. He actually believes that he is the real deal and is going to lay a beating on the champion. The disconnection from reality demonstrated by the bully is amazing. They live in a very small world and believe they are in complete control. But their world is about to be rocked.

What happens next makes you giddy with delight. For two rounds – 6 long painful minutes – the bully gets a taste of his own medicine. He experiences pain, humiliation and ultimately defeat at the hands of a true champion. Justice is served. And, to make it even better, at the end of the "lesson" the bully is typically contrite and repentant. They are given the opportunity to apologize to their victim and try to make things right. Reconciliation begins.

I couldn't watch this and not think about how Jesus – our champion – has defeated the bully of our hearts. Jesus came fully committed to bringing justice. He laid a beatdown on Satan. It wasn't staged and it isn't fake. The enemy has been defeated – his dispatch is still to come – but his authority is gone. We do not need to submit to the bullying of the enemy. In the name of Jesus we can overcome, because He has overcome the enemy.

Our champion has won – the bully has been beatdown.

I Corinthians 15:57

"But thanks be to God! He gives us the victory through our Lord Jesus Christ."

CALLED OUT OF - CALLED INTO.

Fishing – that's what they knew. Nets. Boats. The markets. Hard work. Men working together for long hours to catch and then sell the fish so they could provide for their families. It was probably a good living. Guys working together out in boats on the water. Just being on the water was great on good days, but when the weather was bad it was tough. The community of fishermen was probably a good group of down to earth guys. Sure, there would be a few guys that were hard to get along with, but for the most part a decent bunch of guys.

The Sons of Thunder had quite a business. James and John worked with their dad, Zebedee. They had a number of boats and hired men. Theirs was a thriving business. They were big enough to not simply employ family members, but to have some staff as well. Yes, Sons of Thunder fishing was a going concern. Then Jesus threw a wrench into the family business. He came strolling up the beach and called them to follow Him. How exactly He did that we don't really know. Maybe He had met them earlier and they had chatted a bit. Maybe not. All we know is that at some point in time Jesus came up to them – in the middle of the business day – and called them to follow Him. Leave the business and follow Me.

What does that mean? What would we do? Where would we go? How would we make money? Can I keep fishing? I don't really know you – who are you? Can I trust you? What is all this about? I am sure they had lots of unanswered questions. They had a very clear understanding of what they were called out of. However, they could see very little of what they were being called into.

I recently experienced something like this. I believed that the Lord was asking me to walk away from my business of 13 years. He was calling me out of my marketing agency and into…what? That was the problem. I could see very clearly what I would be walking away from, but I couldn't really see what the Lord was leading me into. Sure, I had longings and desires deep in my heart that I believed the Lord wanted to call me into, but what was the plan? Can I trust you? What will I be doing? How will I make money? What is all this about? Yes, I can empathize with James and John.

Some of you may be sensing the Lord calling you out of something you know well into something you don't know very well. It doesn't have to be your work or career, but it could be. Don't be dismayed if you don't see clearly what you think the Lord is calling you into. That's the plan. He always calls us out of something in order to call us into something. The uncertainty forces us to trust Him. It takes faith. We must believe that He is good; that He loves us; that He will provide for all our needs; that He knows us and is leading us deeper into His heart in us and through us. Look at James and John – their willingness to step into the unknown changed the course of history.

He will call you "out of" in order to call you "into" – follow Him in faith.

Mark 1:19, 20

"When He had gone a little farther, He saw James Son of Zebedee and his brother John in a boat, preparing their nets. Without delay He called them, and they left their father Zebedee in the boat with the hired men and followed Him."

CAN I PRAY FOR YOU?

Strangers in Starbucks.

A buddy on my boat.

A good friend in my office.

A client on the phone.

A pastor up a mountain.

A new acquaintance at a church meeting.

What do all these people have in common? Well, I have had the privilege and pleasure of praying for them at various times over the past week.

It's quite simple really. I find myself talking with people who are facing challenges of all kinds: starting a new business, moving cities, the rigors of everyday life, marriage troubles, job loss, health issues, stresses of all sorts…basically dealing with the stuff of life. When we finish talking I ask a very simple, yet powerful question,

"Can I pray for you?"

I have decided that as often as possible, and whenever appropriate, I will finish my interaction with someone by praying for them. Most times these people are Jesus followers, but sometimes they are not. In all the times I have done this throughout the years I have only had one person say "no". So, I simply said that's ok, and prayed for them at another time when I was alone.

Do you struggle sometimes with how you can make a difference, how you can be a kingdom builder, a marketplace minister? Well, I have found that this is a simple, yet profound and powerful way to touch people's lives and facilitate the work of the Holy Spirit. Care enough to ask questions and listen to people, then ask if you can pray for them.

Now, I am not a prayer expert by any means, but I have had the privilege of being taught and mentored by men who are powerful prayers. What I do know is this: God responds to prayer. By some incredible grace amidst his divine omnipotence, and omniscience the Lord of All has chosen to "limit" himself to our prayers. God has chosen to invite and engage us in His plans and purposes by asking us to ask Him. Wow. I know, it sounds crazy – part of how we partner with the Sovereign Lord in His purposes is to pray. Listen, commune, and ask.

When we pray God moves. When we pray the spirit realm shifts. When we pray the purposes of God are released and things happen. I am no incredible man of faith and power, but many, many times people have said to me, "Wow, I really appreciated it when you prayed for me – my heart was really touched." Is that because of my awesomely orated prayerful expression? No, my simple sentiments synergize with the all-powerful God who sets things in motion and moves in the heart of the focus of my petition.

This is awesome, men. How can we make a powerful and profound impact in people's lives? Pray for them. Ask them for permission to do so and do it right there out loud – let them hear you. Don't make a scene, be discreet, but be verbal.

So, what to pray? How to pray? Well, here is what I do: I basically try to pray scripture. I thank God for how much He loves them, how He will never leave them, how they are not alone, how the Lord will provide for all their needs – I affirm God's care and love. Then I ask the Lord to meet them where they are – whatever that may look like: to provide encouragement, strength, hope, faith, resources, freedom, revelation, a job, etc. I may do spiritual warfare and bring the cross of Christ between them and the strategy of the enemy. I thank the Lord for this person and who He has created, crafted and called them to be. I also always pray that God's Kingdom would come and His will would be done in them and through them.

I will also listen in my spirit for something specific the Lord may be asking me to pray or share – a scripture, a picture, a lesson, etc. Then I share that too. So, I listen in my spirit for some direction from the Lord and I pray scriptures. Simple, really. But the impact is profound because of the work of the Holy Spirit.

So guys, let's go for it. Let's commit to being prayer ministers. Let's commit to engaging with and listening to people – friends, family, strangers, employees, co-workers, etc – and simply then love on them through prayer. The miracle of prayer is what God does in the heart of the person for whom we pray – and that's very cool to see.

This great adventure starts with a simple question, "Can I pray for you?"

Go for it.

Ephesians 6:18
"And pray in the Spirit on all occasions with all kinds of prayers and requests. With this in mind, be alert and always keep on praying for all the Lord's people."

James 5:16
"...the prayer of a righteous person is powerful and effective."

Mark 11:24
"Therefore I tell you, whatever you ask for in prayer, believe that you have received it, and it will be yours."

CAN I TRUST YOU?

"Honey, there is smoke coming out from underneath the dash!"

Uh oh, that is not good.

Anne and I were enjoying a beautiful sunset cruise on Okanagan Lake in my old wood boat. The sun was shining; the water was like glass; a little wine, cheese and crackers and we were having a great relaxing time together. The sun was setting so we thought it was time to head back to Kelowna.

That's when things started to go sideways...

I smelled burning plastic - as did Anne. Anne spotted the smoke coming out from underneath the dash. I stopped the engine and crawled under for a look. My Amp meter had started ping-ponging back and forth right before the burning smell, so I focused in on that wiring. Sure enough, the wiring was red hot and the casing was melting. I tried to pull it free and sparks started to fly. I felt down the main wiring harness going back to the engine and it was beginning to melt as well.

I opened up the engine box to get a look at what was going on in there and was met with significant amounts of billowing smoke. The main wiring harness on the top of the engine was now melted. I had a fire extinguisher, but knew that if I did not eliminate the short we would soon be on fire and perhaps experience an explosion when spark/fire meets with gas fumes.

I disconnected the positive lead from the battery and everything stopped.

So, to cut a very long story short, we had to be rescued from way up the lake, I have had to put all new wiring in my boat, as well as fix my generator and install a new voltage regulator. My generator malfunctioned and blew the voltage regulator, which caused a surge and a short, etc., etc.

I found myself asking the Lord what He was trying to teach me, because as some of you know, my boat has not been without its issues. I began to see a little lesson emerge after I got my repaired boat back and headed out on the water again...

Trust.

Can I really trust this boat? Can I enjoy our time on the water without always carrying a sense of impending doom? When I am out in the boat do I hold my breath as it were, waiting for something else to go wrong? Will I allow myself to lose the joy of being out on the water with my Father in a boat that I love being in? Or, can I trust God in the midst of troubles?

Trust is earned, and trust is given. When someone, or something, breaks our trust by letting us down it is wise to not simply give all of our trust back to them. Trust is earned as someone, or something, proves trustworthy. The trouble is, how much does it take to earn your trust back? At some point in time we have to choose to trust again.

I got an email from a young lady last week who had been going through a rough time on a number of fronts. What she said about what the Lord is teaching her in the midst of it is quite profound:

"Not to sound negative, but tough things happen and life is always going to be full of ups and downs and curve balls -- that's just how it is. But it's learning to see all of life (the good and the not so good) as a progressive journey that we walk through that makes a difference; that all of life is a gift from God, and He walks with you every step of the way, so you might as well stop living in survival mode. *Living* life begins when you learn to enjoy where you're at on the way to where you're going, instead of just 'existing' from crisis to crisis."

Whether someone, or perhaps you feel God Himself, has let you down you must choose to trust again and not simply exist from crisis to crisis – living in a sense of impending doom. Life will not be perfect this side of heaven, things will go wrong, people will let us down, and God will not always do what we think He should do. However, God is an ever present help in times of trouble when people or things let you down. And, He is the only firm foundation we can stand upon. We must choose to trust again.

Yes, trust is earned, but trust is also given. Choose to trust again – don't simply exist from crisis to crisis.

Psalm 22:4, 5

"In you our fathers put their trust; they trusted you and you delivered them. They cried to you and were saved; in you they trusted and were not disappointed."

Psalm 46:1

"God is our refuge and strength, an ever-present help in trouble."

Psalm 27:13

"I remain confident of this: I will see the goodness of the LORD in the land of the living."

CAN'T IS A SWEAR WORD

When our sons were little we taught them that "Can't is a swear word." As much as we were able to we wanted them never to use the word "can't". 'Can't' is such a faithless word.

I remember one time when the boys were very young we did a simple hike up to the top of a small mountain behind our home. At the top of the mountain we found lots of flagstone and began to build various structures out of these rocks. David was working feverishly on an elaborate creation when it began to fall apart – he had to build it all over again. As he sat looking at the pile of rocks that 5 seconds earlier was very near to being his completed masterpiece, he said out loud to himself, "I can do all things through Christ who gives me strength." He then started to rebuild his creation.

Wow, he was getting it, and for him at this moment the rubber of his faith and belief was hitting the road. He was asking the Lord to help him get on with the job of rebuilding. The strength he needed, the patience he needed, the self-control he needed, the hope he needed; he was looking to the Lord to provide him with this because he knew he couldn't do it on his own.

You see, the reality is that apart from Christ we can do nothing. Apart from Christ 'can't' is a perpetual state of being. Everything that we are was spoken into being by Him. He knit us together in our mother's womb. The miracle of thought, emotion, movement, speech, foresight, insight, wisdom, etc. is all because of the wonder of His creation. Every cell of our being, every atom of this earth is from Him, to Him and through Him. Wow – not only can we 'do' nothing apart from Him, but we 'are' nothing apart from Him.

Sadly, however, many of us try to live life apart from Him. Not that we don't want Him in our lives and don't love Him. No, we simply just go about the activities of our daily lives in our own strength. We do not acknowledge that we are nothing without Him and can do nothing without Him – and, therefore, can do all things through Him. We seem to put on our war face, put our head down and pound through whatever difficulty we are facing only to realize sometime into the battle that we are losing ground and this difficulty is killing us. We then cry out to God for help.

Each and every minute of every day we need to live with an ongoing sense of gratitude and awe that we 'are' and we 'do' only because of the wonder of God's work in us. We can then freely and boldly boast that we can do nothing apart from Christ, and that we can subsequently do all things through Christ who strengthens us.

If you are facing issues in your life that are overwhelming you, make sure that you find your strength in Christ. Come to Him and surrender. Ask for and then receive all the strength, hope, patience, longsuffering, wisdom, self-control, etc. that you need to walk where He is leading you.

Remember, apart from Him you can do nothing, but you can do all things through Christ who gives you strength.

Philippians 4:13

"I can do all things through Christ who gives me strength."

CHRISTIAN ATHEISM

God takes initiative. He actually makes the first move. It is easy, though, in the midst of our lives to think that it all depends on you. You have to make it happen. There is an old adage that says, "If it is to be, it's up to me." There is some truth in that. We do have a role to play. However, we must remember that God is alive and engaged. He is not some uninvolved, detached being off in never-never land looking on passively to see if we get it right.

I have realized that it is easy for me to go about my life busily trying to carry all my God-given responsibilities – husband, father, brother, leader, follower – gutting it out, trying to do the best that I can. Sure, I ask the Lord to lead and guide me, to give me wisdom and strength to do what He has asked me to do, but do I really believe that He will move on my behalf without being asked to by me? Or does He only move because I have done something to earn His favour, or catch His attention?

I call this Christian Atheism – knowing Jesus, believing in Him, following Him, but not truly believing that He is alive and well and that He takes initiative in my life. Not truly believing that He loves me and delights in me and that He will be actively involved in my life – by His initiative. Not believing that He will surprise me with His love, and not simply respond to my "faithfulness".

When I was 9, the Lord miraculously saved my life after I was run over by a car on the highway at Whistler. He broke into my life and called me to follow Him. I didn't ask for that. He chose me. He initiated this relationship. And, He has continued to take initiative in my life for over 35 years.

He did the same for you. He called you and He continues to call you. He continues to take initiative in your life. He does this because He loves you and delights in you.

Don't fall into the trap of Christian Atheism – God calls you, He initiates because He loves you. It's not all up to you.

John 15: 16
"You did not choose me, but I chose you and appointed you to go and bear fruit—fruit that will last. Then the Father will give you whatever you ask in my name."

COMMUNITY IS CRITICAL

Have you ever been to a social event where you didn't know anyone? It can be a little awkward, can't it? Or, it can be a little adventurous...Who will you meet? What can you learn? What interesting people are here that you would never otherwise have the opportunity to connect with?

A few months ago I found myself in this very scenario. I was working with a client in Atlantic Canada to whom I had spoken on the phone a few times, but never met prior to this encounter. We spent the day together as I trained his staff and that evening he invited me to a surprise birthday party for a close friend of his. I initially declined because I figured I would feel out of place, and people would wonder who the new guy was in the corner and why he crashed the party. He explained to me that there would be over 100 people at the party and I would fit right in. This changed things, so I figured it would be a great opportunity to meet and party with some friendly eastern Canadians.

So, that evening I found myself amidst scores of partiers enjoying live music, great food and beverage, and who were there to celebrate the life of their dear friend who, by the stories shared by many in attendance, had spent his 50 years making other people's lives better. I felt honored and privileged to witness the community this man had built by caring for others. It made me think, who would be at a party like this for me? Have I invested my life in a way that has created community and made other people's lives better?

I ended up chatting with a certain man for an extended period of time. It turns out he was a very well-known and influential politician. He has enjoyed a long and significant career in provincial politics having served as Minister of Finance, Minister of Education and other powerful positions of authority. We talked about community, change, the political process and politics in general. I judged him to be a man of high moral standards and one who truly wants to work for the good of society. He began to encourage me to run for office and spoke very highly of the good that I could accomplish through the political process. He pointed out how my background, character, skills and abilities have positioned me to be successful in the world of politics. I thanked him for his kind encouragement and began to ask him about the nasty elements of politics and the toll it takes on someone who truly wants to make a difference.

I asked him a specific question, "How do you maintain your vision and motivation to create positive political change in the midst of oftentimes ruthless, vicious, unfair and selfish political opposition." His answer caught my attention...

"By surrounding myself with likeminded, good people who will stand together in the midst of the opposition reminding me why we are doing this", he replied.

Wow - so simple, yet so profound. I immediately saw how this was relevant, not just to those in politics, but to all of us. I would call what he was talking about a "band of brothers", or a community of allies. Sadly, most men feel like "abandoned brothers" and not part of a band of brothers. But you know something? We can't expect community to somehow magically form and then invite us in with open arms. No, we must create community.

We must take the initiative to make community happen. We must choose to reach out and connect with other men. We must choose to meet together regularly, cultivating deep, open and honest relationships as allies in this adventure called the Kingdom of God. Like Clint Eastwood said, "A man alone is easy prey." Similar to my new political friend we are the targets of ruthless, vicious, unfair and selfish opposition that we cannot withstand alone – we need each other. We must walk together as one in a community of allies.

Have you chosen to surround yourself with likeminded, good men who will walk with you in the midst of opposition and remind you why we are doing this? If you have not, it is never too late. Community is critical and it must be created. Take the initiative and create a community of allies to help keep you envisioned and engaged in this adventure of walking with Jesus. We are not meant to walk alone. We must be united – in community - walking together as one.

John17:11, 21, 22, 23
"I will remain in the world no longer, but they are still in the world and I and coming to you. Holy Father, protect them by the power of your name – the name you gave me – so that they may be one as we are one...that all of them may be one...I have given them the glory that you gave me, that they may be one as we are one; I in them and you in me. May they be brought to complete unity..."

COURAGE IS NOT A GIFT

John Wayne. An iconic man's man. I remember the first time I saw a John Wayne movie when I was a boy. True Grit. It was the late 60's and my dad took us to the 17th St. Drive In, in Calgary. We had an old wood paneled Ford station wagon - sleeping bags in the back for when we fell asleep. I'll never forget watching John Wayne fearlessly gallop across the clearing toward his enemies: the reins of his horse in his mouth, lever action Winchester blasting away in his right hand and his six shooter blasting in his left. Wow. Now that's a man. Fearless.

At least I thought he was fearless. I have since learned John Wayne's definition of courage – "Being scared spitless, but saddling up anyways." It's been said there are two kinds of people in this world: those who are afraid and those who are afraid. No one is fearless. You see, it's what we do with the fear that matters. That's where we separate the men from the boys. Fear is the prerequisite for courage. Courage is not the absence of fear, but the willingness to keep going in spite of it. Courage is not a gift; it is a decision to keep going even though you are afraid.

We all have an equal opportunity to be courageous, because courage is an act of your will. The greatest gift God has given mankind is our ability to choose – our will. Even though you're afraid, maybe terrified, you can choose to keep going. You can choose to press through your fears. Surrender your fears to God and don't let them stop you. Press on. If you're afraid, then you have the opportunity to be courageous.

God didn't say to Joshua that He would give him courage. He told him to be strong and courageous. In other words, He told him to "choose" to be strong and courageous. Give your fear to God and make a decision to keep moving forward – that's courage.

Courage is not a gift - it's being scared spitless, but saddling up anyway.

Joshua 1:9
"Have I not commanded you? Be strong and courageous. Do not be terrified; do not be discouraged, for the LORD your God will be with you wherever you go."

DEPTHS OF DESIRE

"Ogres are like onions – they have layers."

And so Shrek tries to explain that there is more to ogres than what most people think. There is a depth to them that nobody really understands.

I think desire is like that too. Desire has layers – let's call them depths. We have deep desires and we have shallow desires. Shallow desires are those desires that are close to the surface and are the easiest to be aware of. Deep desires are those desires that may be a little more difficult to be aware of because they are found deep in our hearts. Let me give you an example where this became very clear to me.

I was working late one night at my office. I was all alone. I was tired. I was lonely. I wasn't feeling particularly valuable, significant or strong. Are you getting this picture? Can you see where it's leading? In the midst of this the name of a website pops into my mind. I have no idea where I heard this website name. All I know is that it pops into my mind and I can't get it outta there. I know this website is probably pornographic, and populated with photos of beautiful naked women. I want to go there. I want to see what's there. I want to see beautiful naked women. I keep resisting the urge to type in the URL, but the desire to go to this website keeps growing.

As you know, God created women as the beautiful crowning glory of creation and there is a beauty to women that is very desirable. I wanted to look at beautiful women. This was a "shallow" desire for me at this particular point in time, but I knew that there was a "deeper" pure desire in my heart. The shallow desire that I was experiencing was not a pure desire. I knew that this desire would lead to sin. I would be captivated by lust. A moment's pleasure would lead to imprisonment. Satisfying this shallow desire would ultimately impact my deeper desire for a deep, rich, intimate and pure relationship with my wife and with my Lord.

Guys, I know that you know this temptation. We face it on a regular basis. I did not want to give in to this shallow desire. So, this is what I did. I spoke out loud to the Lord. I was very honest and I told Him that I really wanted to look at this website. I confessed my "shallow" desire to the Lord. However, I then confessed my "deep" desire to the Lord. I told Him that what I really wanted was a pure, passionate, loving, intimate and deep relationship with my wife. I told Him that I also really wanted a pure, passionate, loving, intimate and deep relationship with Him.

You know what happened? My shallow desire left. It vanished. My deep desire took precedence. I no longer wanted to look at that website. Wow. I thanked the Lord for His goodness, finished my work and went home – free.

We need to be aware of our deep desires and express them to the Lord. That simple act can enable us to overcome shallow desires that can seem so overwhelming in the moment.

Proverbs 20:5

"The purposes of a man's heart are deep waters, but a man of understanding draws them out."

DIVER OR DABBLER?

I got together for dinner with a very good buddy of mine recently. I've known this man for over 30 years, and we've experienced a lot of life together. As we ate dinner on the outdoor patio of an ocean side restaurant the sun began setting and cast a beautifully, brilliant orange glow across the sky.

"Oh man, I wish I had my camera."

And with the zeal of a high-priced professional photographer my friend waxed eloquently about how he would shoot this scene. Background shadows, foreground elements, light tones, camera angles - you name it - and I could tell these things were running through his mind at a million miles an hour. However, my friend is not a high-priced professional photographer. Nope, he has a very significant, high-profile position completely unrelated to anything photographic.

You see, he had recently taken up a very cool hobby – a certain style of photography called HDR Photography. He has bought all of the camera and computer equipment necessary to excel at this hobby. He has spent hours studying this technique on the internet and has invested probably hundreds of hours practicing by taking thousands of photos – many of them from a helicopter. He has even studied other photo artists as a means of inspiring himself onto greater accomplishments.

As my friend passionately talked about his newfound hobby I realized that what I was seeing in him is a character trait that I have witnessed in him for 3 decades: My friend is a diver, not a dabbler. When he gets into something he wholeheartedly dives in. He researches, studies, talks to people, investigates, practices, accumulates, purchases, networks – he does whatever it takes to become a great proficient. I have always admired this about him. When he leaps into something he leaps in wholeheartedly. He definitely does not dabble. You know what dabbling is - trying something out just a little. Not too much commitment. Stick your toe in the water per se and see if the waters are pleasant or not. Nope, not Tim. He dives right in. If something is worth doing, then it's worth doing wholeheartedly to the best of your ability.

I wish I was more like that. Are you like that? Do you know anybody like that - a diver not a dabbler? I think of Stephen Curtis Chapman's song called "Dive":

"I'm divin' in, I'm goin' deep. In over my head I want to be. Caught in the rush. Lost in the flow. In over my head I want to go. The river's deep, the river's wide, the river's water is alive. So sink or swim I'm divin' in."

So, when it comes to Jesus are you a diver or a dabbler? Are you diving into total trust, total submission, and total obedience to Jesus? Or, are you dabbling? Get just enough of Jesus to make you feel good. Don't get too close to get convicted and have to make some significant changes in your life. Don't get too serious about this whole Jesus thing – you don't want to have to totally change things around. Keep doing all that stuff that makes you feel good and mix in a little "church", a little "religion" to keep your wife off your back – or keep your conscience clear for a little bit of time.

No, Jesus did not call us to be dabblers. He was all about diving in. Wholeheartedness. Totally committed. Abandonment. Hot or cold – not lukewarm. No dabbling.

Let's do it. Let's dive in and wholeheartedly abandon our lives to Jesus – imagine what He could do with divers who aren't dabbling anymore...

Revelation 3:15-17
"I know your deeds that you are neither cold nor hot. I wish you were either one or the other. So, because you are lukewarm – neither hot nor cold – I am about to spit you out of my mouth. You say, 'I am rich; I have acquired wealth and do not need a thing.' But you do not realize that you are wretched, pitiful, poor, blind and naked."

DO NOTHING WELL

Our marriage began with a beautiful honeymoon on the island of Kauai in the Hawaiian Islands. We had a wonderful time together and learned much about each other. One of the things we learned was that Anne and I like to holiday differently.

Do you and your wife like to holiday differently? I think we tend to like to holiday in one of two ways: some people like to take it easy, rest, read some books and do nothing – that would be my wife. Now, that doesn't mean that she doesn't like doing some adventures and having a little excitement, but by and large she would prefer rest to activity. Other people like to be very active. They like lots of adventure with each new day being something new – that would be me. Not that I can't rest, relax and do nothing, but I don't "do nothing well".

How do you like to holiday? Are you into rest or action? One is not better than the other, they are simply different.

As I mentioned, we discovered this difference on our honeymoon. So, when we ended up in Los Cabos for our 15th anniversary we were prepared to accept each other as is – free to be you. We arrived at our resort; we each grabbed a book and headed to the palapa by the pool. We both started reading. After 45 minutes I closed my book and said, "Let's go do something!" Anne looked at me incredulously and said, "We've only been here for 30 minutes." I then said, "It's been 45 minutes – I was timing it."

She then communicated in no uncertain terms that I was free to live the adventure and shake my sillies out, but she was going to keep reading. So, I headed off on a great cycling adventure with Jesus to the next village over.

In a previous How's The Viz? I talked about living in the green light, waiting for the red light instead of the other way around. I think this only works if we can also "do nothing well" and simply "be". In other words, we know how to be still; we know how to rest; we can do nothing and not have it drive us crazy. I have mellowed out over the last 10 years, but I still don't do nothing as well as I would like to. Like holidaying, we each have different propensities – some have a propensity to be over active, and some under active. Some of us need to learn how to get off our derrieres and get to work. Some of us need to learn to put the brakes on and take it easy – chill out and learn to do nothing well. Learn to "be" and not just "do".

I don't think doing nothing well solely means sitting there with eyes closed in total silence focused on nothing in particular, but it could be that. I think doing nothing well involves being at peace in stillness and simplicity; not being intimidated by solitude and silence; and being patient when God has us wait or when He puts up a red light. It's resting in Jesus and quieting our hearts. It has to do with trust. Do we trust God with everything? A key to effectively living in the green and waiting for the red is learning to do nothing well, rest, be quiet and simply "be".

Learn to do nothing well – rest and "be" quiet. Fully put your trust in Jesus and you will find new strength.

Isaiah 30:15

"This is what the Sovereign LORD, the Holy One of Israel, says: "In repentance and rest is your salvation, in quietness and trust is your strength, but you would have none of it."

DO YOU BELIEVE I CAN STILL PART THE WATERS?

HELP!!!!!!!!! Have you ever prayed a deep, guttural prayer that comes out of the pit of your stomach motivated by an overwhelming, paralyzing fear? Well, this was one of those.

Anne and I and our 2 "toddler" sons had recently left Winnipeg to move back to BC. I had been working with the Winnipeg Jets, who were now going to Phoenix. Anne and I believed that the Lord was leading us back to BC. I had spent a lot of time during my last year with the hockey club cultivating an employment opportunity with a Kelowna organization. They had indicated to me that they wanted to hire me to start a program I had presented to them. There were a few details to work out, but they were excited to bring me on.

So, with faith in our hearts that the Lord was calling us to Kelowna, and the assurance of this organization that they were intending to hire me, we sold our home and shipped all our belongings to Kelowna. We headed to Langley for a few weeks to stay with Anne's parents.

After we had been at Anne's parent's place for 4 weeks I got the call that the deal was off. I was gutted. Winded. Devastated. How could God let this happen? We were following Him – He was supposed to provide. I went for a desperate prayer walk with the Lord and prayed that gut honest one word prayer – help! I felt like we were the Israelites who had been led out of Egypt only to be trapped at the Red Sea, waiting to be slaughtered by Pharaoh's economic army.

That's when the Lord asked me, "Do you believe I can still part waters?"

I knew I had no option. I had to believe that He can still part waters, or we were dead. It was at that point that He told me to start my own company. Through lots of hard work and the faithfulness of God, MacLean Group has been a wonderful blessing for many years. However, it all began with a belief that God still parts waters.

Do you believe that God can part the waters in your situation? He can. Believe and follow Him.

Exodus 14: 13, 14

"Moses answered the people, 'Do not be afraid. Stand firm and you will see the deliverance the LORD will bring you today. The Egyptians you see today you will never see again. The LORD will fight for you; you need only to be still.'"

DO YOU GIVE?

Remember when you used to play fight and wrestle with your friends or family when you were a boy? Inevitably someone would get put into a painful position of some kind – perhaps you – and the key question would be asked, "Do you give?"

Say Uncle, give up, give in, surrender, submit, tap out – there are lots of different ways to say it, but it all means the same. Do you give up? Do you admit that you have been beaten? Do you choose to recognize the superiority of the one asking the question? No one liked admitting it, but we all had to at some point in time.

My brother is 10 years older than me. We would play fight when I was a kid and he was a young adult. It was always no contest – I would submit every time. His favorite move was to get me on my back and then pull my legs up over my head so I was curled up in a ball on the back of my neck staring at my chest, barely able to breathe. He would then ask me the question, "Do you give?" "Yes, yes, yes – I give, I give I give." He would let me go and laugh. I had submitted to his superiority. It made me so mad! I hated that feeling.

I met Jesus as a preteen – through my brother after he met Jesus. It took into my late 20s though to begin to really understand that Jesus was beckoning me to totally surrender to him. He was asking me to surrender my hopes, dreams, expectations, aspirations and plans. This life is not about Jesus blessing my plans, but me surrendering mine to Him and walking wholeheartedly with Him where He leads me – which may be into the very hopes, dreams and plans that are in my heart, but not until my heart is surrendered to Him first.

It took me a long time to surrender. Jesus kept inviting me to voluntarily surrender, but I wasn't really getting the point. So, He enrolled me in the school of brokenness and submission. Over the course of 7 years He lovingly, yet ruthlessly, broke my will, plans, dreams, hopes, expectations and aspirations – only to generously and graciously fulfill many, many of them after I had truly surrendered and submitted to Him.

There is resurrection only after death. The way to life in Jesus is to submit to die so that we might live. If we lose our life we shall find it. If we seek to find our life we shall lose it. Death of a vision precedes the resurrection of a vision. When we come to Jesus He asks us to submit and surrender our will to Him - to give up our plans for His. Sadly, many of us when we hear the words "submit" and "surrender" think back to negative experiences we may have had when we were younger. We then resist, or begrudgingly submit. We lay down our lives, but in our hearts we are still standing up.

Surrender and submission to Jesus is absolutely critical to discovering the life that He has for us. If we do not submit – out of His great love for us – He will begin to turn the heat up in our lives to lead us to surrender to Him. Truly surrendering our will, heart, dreams, hopes, plans, expectations and aspirations – death to self – leads to true life in Jesus.

He loves you enough to turn up the heat in your life to lead you to surrender to Him. The question is, "Do you give?"

Matthew 10:39
"Whoever finds his life will lose it, and whoever loses his life for my sake will find it."

DON'T BACK DOWN

The wind was howling down the mountainside like a freight train. Rain and sleet were pounding our faces and stinging our eyes to the point where our vision was impaired. Painstakingly we trudged onward in the face of this violent opposition – one foot in front of the other, gradually climbing up the mountain ever so slowly.

The weather conditions were definitely having an impact on my motivation. I really didn't want to be here – I was getting too old for this kind of thing. I would rather be in a luxury mountain resort somewhere, sitting outside in a hot tub with the snowflakes gently drifting down to create a heavenly serene moment of winter bliss while I'm moving ever so effortlessly into greater and greater degrees of relaxation and comfort.

But that was out of the question, totally impossible right now and would defeat the whole purpose of this exercise. You see, my son Benjamin and I were on the last leg of his transition from boyhood into young manhood. We were in the middle of the backcountry of the Upper Cascade Mountains at 10,000 ft. climbing to the top of the peaks in Cathedral Lakes Provincial Park in "Supernatural" British Columbia.

This was supposed to be hard. It was supposed to test his strength. It was supposed to be demanding and demotivating. It was all designed to cause him to reach the end of the strength he thought he had and then dig deeper to discover a manly strength of body, soul and spirit that he didn't know he had. However, it wasn't supposed to do that for me…

So, here we were hiking and climbing head long into a violent opposition causing us to question our quest, turn around, and run home for comfort and convenience. If we had done that it would have scarred both of us for the rest of our lives.

I needed to give myself a pep talk and pass it on to Benjamin. So I talked about choosing to not back down and the need to get violent sometimes. I talked about how this wind and sleet were violent opposition attempting to dissuade us from our objective, but men dig deep in times like these and don't give up. We don't surrender, we don't back down. When the going gets tough, men get going.

And, sometimes it helps to engage our hearts by engaging our tongues. Declare your intentions, declare your convictions, and declare your beliefs – vehemently and violently. In other words, do it with great might, force and fury. Subsequently we yelled at the wind. We screamed our faces off. We told the wind and sleet in no-uncertain-terms that we would not be dissuaded, we would not back down and we would not quit.

And you know what? Our hearts shifted. We were not somber and sour. We were not demotivated and downcast. We were not weak and whimpering. We had a newfound boldness, strength, motivation and focus. We charged up the mountainside with each new step being a step into greater freedom.

King David understood this principle. The Psalms are filled with this kind of "self-talk" and declaration. He would regularly speak to himself and to the emotions that were opposing him in order to encourage himself to step into greater faith – into the truth of the greatness of God.

Let's follow King David's example and speak to our souls, speak to our hearts and don't back down. If you are considering backing down from what you believe the Lord is leading you in – don't. Don't back down in the face of opposition. Any advancement of God's kingdom in you and through you will be met with opposition. Part of the purpose of that is to discover a greater strength in God than perhaps you didn't know you had.

So, don't back down. Keep going. Keep moving forward vehemently speaking truth to your heart to resist the opposition set against you. The Kingdom needs you.

Psalm 42:10, 11
"My bones suffer mortal agony as my foes taunt me, saying to me all day long, "Where is your God?" Why, my soul, are you downcast? Why so disturbed within me? Put your hope in God, for I will yet praise him, my Savior and my God."

Psalm 43:4, 5
"Then I will go to the altar of God, to God, my joy and my delight. I will praise you with the lyre, O God, my God. Why, my soul, are you downcast? Why so disturbed within me? Put your hope in God, for I will yet praise him, my Savior and my God."

DON'T FORGET TO BREATHE

All middle-aged, overweight, out of shape men raise your hand. Ah yes, there are quite a few of us. We are at that stage of life, aren't we? You know… a little bit rounder in the mid-section. A little more chin. A little less able to keep up with our kids. My dad used to say, "That must be jelly, 'cause jam don't shake like that." Yes, there is a little more jelly than usual. Don't worry though, it's only natural. And, that's the problem. It will continue to grow if we don't do something to change the natural flow of things. And for you younger guys – it's coming. I used to have 6% body fat too…

So, I have started to make a change. I am at a gym 3 times a week to do some exercise and change the natural course of things. I want to be able to keep up with my sons. I want to be able to enjoy the activities that I don't love as much now because they are far more difficult than they used to be. I even have a personal trainer who has worked with me to put a program together. No great changes yet, but I'm on the right road. During our first session he said something to me that has continued to resonate.

"Don't forget to breathe."

It seems a little silly doesn't it? Who is going to forget to breathe? Well, a common error with people who are exercising is that they forget to breathe. They hold their breath. They are concentrating so much on the exercise that they actually hold their breath and forget to breathe. If they continue to do so, they will pass out. I am concentrating on my breathing while I exercise to ensure that I breathe regularly and deeply to get the most benefit out of my training.

I think in life we can also forget to breathe. We can actually be too busy to breathe. We are working hard to carry all of our responsibilities and we don't breathe properly. We simply hold our breath and work hard to make it through. If we keep doing that we will ultimately pass out. Some of you may be feeling out of breath. Some of you may be feeling light headed and ready to pass out.

It's time to breathe.

So, how do we breathe? I don't think it necessarily means we need to drop what we are carrying. Though, there may be some of you who are carrying too much. I think it means we choose to breathe in the midst of the work. Quiet your heart and breathe in God's love. Breathe in His peace. Breathe in His hope. Breathe in His rest. Breathe in His Holy Spirit. We need to still our hearts in the midst of the busyness and look to God for our provision of hope, grace, strength and encouragement.

Don't forget to breathe in God's heart for you.

Psalm 46:10, 11
"Be still, and know that I am God; I will be exalted among the nations, I will be exalted in the earth. The LORD Almighty is with us; the God of Jacob is our fortress."

DON'T RIDE A ONE-PEDAL BICYCLE

My first "cool" bike was a Sears Spider 3. Three speeds. Purple, hand brakes, slicks and a big sissy bar. I was the epitome of cool on that bike. Wheelies, cat walks, riding backwards, jumps, skids, riding with no hands – great memories. Of course, there are always the painful memories of endos, tank slappers, hitting parked cars, etc., but we're not going to get into those here.

Remember the feeling of freedom you had as a little boy when you learned to ride a bike without training wheels? Wow. The speed. The freedom. Your world suddenly got far bigger because you could ride a lot farther than you could walk during play time. The power of a two-pedal bicycle was enormous. In fact, what good would a one-pedal bike be?

My point is this: it's amazing the power of 2 pedals working together, but seemingly in complete opposition to each other. When one is up, the other is down. Opposites, but perfectly complementary.

I subscribe to what I call two-pedal theology. For years I rode a one-pedal bike. If there were seemingly oppositional truths, I picked one and rode it hard. I now see that many scriptural truths are the two pedals on the theological bicycle.

A good example? Divine sovereignty and personal responsibility. If all we do is live like everything depends on us, we will become Christian

Atheists. We'll never expect the Lord to sovereignly move without us doing something first. We must also live with a hopeful expectation of His divine sovereignty. He moves powerfully on our behalf – in His sovereignty.

Do we have personal responsibility in how we live and conduct our lives? Yes. Does the Lord respond to how we walk with Him? Yes. However, He also moves sovereignly out of His great goodness and His good greatness. Likewise, if all we do is hope for God to sovereignly move and don't carry any personal responsibility we will never mature, but remain as spiritual babies crying out to be fed and cared for.

The Lord has really leveraged this tough business climate to teach me this truth. I have been working very hard at my business to see it grow and prosper. I have asked the Lord to lead me and guide me. I have asked the Lord to give me wisdom and revelation to know what to do and how to serve Him in and through my business, but I have slowly over the years shifted to riding the personal responsibility pedal. If I don't work hard, the work won't come.

However, these tough economic times have forced me to lean into God's sovereignty. To believe that He will provide for all my needs because He loves me – not because I do all the right things to earn His favour.

I've learned not to ride a one-pedal theological bike – two pedals get you much further.

James 1:17

"*Every good and perfect gift is from above, coming down from the Father of the heavenly lights, who does not change like shifting shadows.*"

DRESS FOR SUCCESS

Clothes. We all wear them. Some of us wear them better than others. Some of us have a good sense of style. Others of us have a style all our own – one perhaps our wives have been trying to change for years. I know for some men clothes are fairly utilitarian. You have to wear some, but you don't really care too much about what you wear. Other men are more intentional about what they wear, wanting to create a certain statement through their attire. Either way, we make a statement by what we wear.

When it comes to clothes and "dressing for success" I have attempted to be fairly intentional. My work requires me to have a certain look. Marketing and communications people are supposed to have a good sense of style – it's expected of us. Throughout the years I have gone from suits and ties, to suits and no ties, to no suits and no ties, to jeans and no ties, shirts tucked in, then untucked – slowly transitioning from conservative to less conservative with my growing age, credibility and confidence.

However, in the last few years I have upped my flamboyant quotient. I discovered a line of shirts that are really quite extraordinary - Bertigo. Bold colors. Bold patterns. Creative stitching. Multiple square buttons. Patterned fabrics on the inside of the collars and cuffs. These shirts make a bold, flamboyant statement. When I brought home my first couple of shirts I got significant ribbing from my wife and sons. Anne said to me, "Do they sell men's clothes where you bought those shirts?" David and

151

Benjamin threatened not to be seen in public with me if I was wearing one of the shirts.

Undeterred by their lack of confidence in my choices, and their lack of style, I have boldly worn these shirts and added numerous others to my wardrobe. In fact, I am now known in many circles for my shirts. A good friend said to me, "Dave, I don't quite understand you. You are a man's man, but you wear shirts like *that*." Anne has actually named my shirts: Mango Salsa, Key Lime Pie, Coconut Crème, Aqua Velva, Pixel, Pajama, etc. Every time I wear these shirts I get compliments from people. The gal at Starbucks, a client at a trade show, a server in a restaurant, a stranger in a hotel lobby, even our plumber – I get comments all the time typically along the lines of, "I love that shirt." And, I have to confess, I really enjoy the comments that these shirts elicit. I love making a bold statement with my presence.

As I was lying in bed one Saturday getting ready to get up and head off to a sale to get a couple more shirts, the Lord reminded me that I should be more concerned about how I clothe my heart, than by how I clothe my body. Do I care as much about my inner man as I do about my outer man? Do I take as much care and attention in clothing my heart as I do in clothing my body? If I really want to dress for success then my primary concern should be clothing my heart in godliness, compassion, love, humility, grace, mercy, wisdom, etc. That doesn't mean that we can't wear some pretty sharp clothes as well, but our heart needs to be our primary concern.

So men, let's truly dress for success by clothing our hearts in Christ; focusing on dressing our inner man as well as our outer man.

Colossians 3:12

"Therefore, as God's chosen people, holy and dearly loved, clothe yourselves with compassion, kindness, humility, gentleness and patience."

ABOUT THE AUTHOR

Dave MacLean is a speaker, writer, entrepreneur, husband, father, brother, son and friend. He has spent his career in the marketplace. He believes that full-time ministry is an attitude, not a position and, therefore, sees his work in the business community as ministry.

Dave also loves boating and enjoys spending time alone and with family and friends on the waters of Okanagan Lake in his 1962 Chris Craft mahogany ski boat.

Through the work of Wholehearted Men Dave envisions and equips men to live wholeheartedly in Jesus. Dave's desire is to partner with God to facilitate His breath of life breathing on the dry bones of men's lives, as depicted in Ezekiel 37. Dave delivers one day conferences and three day "boot camps". He has written numerous books and study guides, and also writes a weekly e-visional called "How's The Viz?" – which you can subscribe to.

More information can be found at **www.wholeheartedmen.com.**

Through the work of Wholehearted Leaders Dave also speaks and writes to envision and equip leaders to lead wholeheartedly from a deep sense of identity, conviction, commitment, passion, purpose and life. Dave's desire is to empower socially conscious leaders to lead and live on purpose, from the heart. Dave writes a weekly column and blog for leaders called "ENCOURAGEMENTS".

More information can be found at **www.wholeheartedleaders.com.**

51677431R00093

Made in the USA
Charleston, SC
31 January 2016